The Gospel of Wealth

by

Andrew Carnegie

THE GOSPEL OF WEALTH

The problem of our age is the proper administration of wealth, so that the ties of brotherhood may still bind together the rich and poor in harmonious relationship. The conditions of human life have not only been changed, but revolutionized, within the past few hundred years. In former days there was little difference between the dwelling, dress, food and environment of the chief and those of his retainers. The Indians are to-day where civilized man then was. When visiting the Sioux, I was led to the wigwam of the chief. It was just like the others in external appearance, and, even within, the difference was trifling between it and those of the poorest of his braves. The contrast between the palace of the millionaire and the cottage of the laborer with us to-day measures the change which has come with civilization.

This change, however, is not to be deplored, but welcomed as highly beneficial. It is well, nay, essential for the progress of the race, that the houses of some should be homes for all that is highest and best in literature and the arts, and for all the refinements of civilization, rather than that none should be so. Much better this great irregularity than universal squalor. Without wealth there can be no Mæcenas. The "good old times" were not good old times. Neither master nor servant was as well situated then as to-day. A relapse to old conditions would be disastrous to both—not the least so to him who serves—and would sweep away civilization with it. But whether the change be for good or ill, it is upon us, beyond our power to alter, and therefore to be accepted and made the best of. It is a waste of time to criticise the inevitable.

It is easy to see how the change has come. One illustration will serve for almost every phase of the cause. In the manufacture of products we have the whole story. It applies to all combinations of human industry, as stimulated and enlarged by the inventions of this scientific age. Formerly articles were manufactured at the domestic hearth or in small shops which formed part of the household. The master and his apprentices worked side by side, the latter living with the master, and therefore subject to the same conditions.

When these apprentices rose to be masters, there was little or no change in their mode of life, and they, in turn, educated in the same routine succeeding apprentices. There was, substantially, social equality, and even political equality, for those engaged in industrial pursuits had then little or no political voice in the State.

But the inevitable result of such a mode of manufacture was crude articles at high prices. To-day the world obtains commodities of excellent quality at prices which even the generation preceding this would have deemed incredible. In the commercial world similar causes have produced similar results, and the race is benefited thereby. The poor enjoy what the rich could not before afford. What were the luxuries have become the necessaries of life. The laborer has now more comforts than the farmer had a few generations ago. The farmer has more luxuries than the landlord had, and is more richly clad and better housed. The landlord has books and pictures rarer, and appointments more artistic, than the King could then obtain.

The price we pay for this salutary change is, no doubt, great. We assemble thousands of operatives in the factory, in the mine, and in the counting-house, of whom the employer can know little or nothing, and to whom the employer is little better than a myth. All intercourse between them is at an end. Rigid Castes are formed, and, as usual, mutual ignorance breeds mutual distrust. Each Caste is without sympathy for the other, and ready to credit anything disparaging in regard to it. Under the law of competition, the employer of thousands is forced into the strictest economies, among which the rates paid to labor figure prominently, and often there is friction between the employer and the employed, between capital and labor, between rich and poor. Human society loses homogeneity.

The price which society pays for the law of competition, like the price it pays for cheap comforts and luxuries, is also great; but the advantages of this law are also greater still, for it is to this law that we owe our wonderful material development, which brings improved conditions in its train. But, whether the law be benign or not, we must say of it, as we say of the change in the conditions of men to which we have referred: It is here; we cannot evade it; no substitutes for it have been found; and while the law may be sometimes hard for the individual, it is best for the race, because it insures the survival of the fittest in every department. We accept and welcome, therefore, as conditions to which we must accommodate ourselves, great inequality of environment, the concentration of business, industrial and commercial, in the hands of a few, and the law of competition between these, as being not only beneficial, but essential for the future progress of the race. Having accepted these, it follows that there must be great scope for the exercise of special ability in the merchant and in the manufacturer who has to conduct affairs upon a great scale. That this talent for organization and management is rare among men is proved by the fact that it invariably secures for its possessor enormous rewards, no matter where or under what laws or conditions. The experienced in affairs always rate the MAN whose services can be obtained as a partner as not only the first consideration, but such as to render the question of his capital scarcely worth considering, for such men soon create capital; while, without the special talent required, capital soon takes wings. Such men become interested in firms or corporations using millions; and estimating only simple interest to be made upon the capital invested, it is inevitable that their income must exceed their expenditures, and that they must accumulate wealth. Nor is there any middle ground which such men can occupy, because the great manufacturing or commercial concern which does not earn at least interest upon its capital soon becomes bankrupt. It must either go forward or fall behind: to stand still is impossible. It is a condition essential for its successful operation that it should be thus far profitable, and even that, in addition to interest on capital, it should make profit. It is a law that men possessed of this peculiar talent for affairs, under the free play of economic forces, must of necessity soon be in receipt of more revenue than can be judiciously expended upon themselves; and this law is as beneficial for the race as the others.

Objections to the foundations upon which society is based are not in order, because the condition of the race is better with these than it has been with any others which have been tried. Of the effect of any new substitutes proposed we cannot be sure. The Socialist or Anarchist who seeks to overturn present conditions is to be regarded as attacking the foundation upon which civilization itself rests, for civilization took its start from the day that the capable, industrious workman said to his incompetent and lazy fellow, "If thou dost not sow, thou shalt not reap," and thus ended primitive Communism by separating the drones from the bees. One who studies this subject will soon be brought face to face with the conclusion that upon the sacred-ness of property civilization itself depends—the right of the laborer to his hundred dollars in the savings-bank, and equally the legal right of the millionaire to his millions. To those who propose to substitute Communism for this intense Individualism the answer, therefore, is: The race has tried that. All progress from that barbarous day to the present time has resulted from its displacement. Not evil, but good, has come to the race from the accumulation of wealth by those who have the ability and energy that produce it. But even if we admit for a moment that it might be better for the race to discard its present foundation, Individualism,—that it is a nobler ideal that man should labor, not for himself alone, but in and for a brotherhood of his fellows, and share with them all in common, realizing Swedenborg's idea of Heaven, where, as he says, the angels derive their happiness, not from laboring for self, but for each other,—even admit all this, and a sufficient answer is, This is not evolution, but revolution. It necessitates the changing of human nature itself—a work of æons, even if it were good to change it, which we cannot know. It is not practicable in our day or in our age. Even if desirable theoretically, it belongs to another and long-succeeding sociological stratum. Our duty is with what is practicable now; with the next step possible in our day and generation. It is criminal to waste our energies in endeavoring to uproot, when all we can profitably or possibly accomplish is to bend the universal tree of humanity a little in the direction most favorable to the production of good fruit under existing circumstances. We might as well urge the destruction of the highest existing type of man because he failed to reach our ideal as to favor the destruction of Individualism, Private Property, the Law of Accumulation of Wealth, and the Law of Competition; for these are the highest results of human experience, the soil in which society so far has produced the best fruit. Unequally or unjustly, perhaps, as these laws sometimes operate, and imperfect as they appear to the Idealist, they are, nevertheless, like the highest type of man, the best and most valuable of all that humanity has yet accomplished.

We start, then, with a condition of affairs under which the best interests of the race are promoted, but which inevitably gives wealth to the few. Thus far, accepting conditions as they exist, the situation can be surveyed and pronounced good. The question then arises,—and, if the foregoing be correct, it is the only question with which we have to deal,—What is the proper mode of administering wealth after the laws upon which civilization is founded have thrown it into the hands of the few? And it is of this great question that I believe I offer the true solution. It will be understood that *fortunes* are here spoken of, not moderate sums saved by many years of effort, the returns from which are required for the comfortable maintenance and education of families. This is not *wealth,* but only *competence,* which it should be the aim of all to acquire.

There are but three modes in which surplus wealth can be disposed of. It can be left to the families of the decedents; or it can be bequeathed for public purposes; or, finally, it can be administered during their lives by its possessors. Under the first and second modes most of the wealth of the world that has reached the few has hitherto been applied. Let us in turn consider each of these modes. The first is the most injudicious. In monarchical countries, the estates and the greatest portion of the wealth are left to the first son, that the vanity of the parent may be gratified by the thought that his name and title are to descend to succeeding generations unimpaired. The condition of this class in Europe to-day teaches the futility of such hopes or ambitions. The successors have become impoverished through their follies or from the fall in the value of land. Even in Great Britain the strict law of entail has been found inadequate to maintain the status of an hereditary class. Its soil is rapidly passing into the hands of the stranger. Under republican institutions the division of property among the children is much fairer, but the question which forces itself upon thoughtful men in all lands is: Why should men leave great fortunes to their children? If this is done from affection, is it not misguided affection? Observation teaches that, generally speaking, it is not well for the children that they should be so burdened. Neither is it well for the state. Beyond providing for the wife and daughters moderate sources of income, and very moderate allowances indeed, if any, for the sons, men may well hesitate, for it is no longer questionable that great sums bequeathed oftener work more for the injury than for the good of the recipients. Wise men will soon conclude that, for the best interests of the members of their families and of the state, such bequests are an improper use of their means.

It is not suggested that men who have failed to educate their sons to earn a livelihood shall cast them adrift in poverty. If any man has seen fit to rear his sons with a view to their living idle lives, or, what is highly commendable, has instilled in them the sentiment that they are in a position to labor for public ends without reference to pecuniary considerations, then, of course, the duty of the parent is to see that such are provided for *in moderation*. There are instances of millionaires' sons unspoiled by wealth, who, being rich, still perform great services in the community. Such are the very salt of the earth, as valuable as, unfortunately, they are rare; still it is not the exception, but the rule, that men must regard, and, looking at the usual result of enormous sums conferred upon legatees, the thoughtful man must shortly say, "I would as soon leave to my son a curse as the almighty dollar," and admit to himself that it is not the welfare of the children, but family pride, which inspires these enormous legacies.

As to the second mode, that of leaving wealth at death for public uses, it may be said that this is only a means for the disposal of wealth, provided a man is content to wait until he is dead before it becomes of much good in the world. Knowledge of the results of legacies bequeathed is not calculated to inspire the brightest hopes of much posthumous good being accomplished. The cases are not few in which the real object sought by the testator is not attained, nor are they few in which his real wishes are thwarted. In many cases the bequests are so used as to become only monuments of his folly. It is well to remember that it requires the exercise of not less ability than that which acquired the wealth to use it so as to be really beneficial to the community. Besides this, it may fairly be said that no man is to be extolled for doing what he cannot help doing, nor is he to be thanked by the community to which he only leaves wealth at death. Men who leave vast sums in this way may fairly be thought men who would not have left it at all had they been able to take it with them. The memories of such cannot be held in grateful remembrance, for there is no grace in their gifts. It is not to be wondered at that such bequests seem so generally to lack the blessing.

The growing disposition to tax more and more heavily large estates left at death is a cheering indication of the growth of a salutary change in public opinion. The State of Pennsylvania now takes—subject to some exceptions —one-tenth of the property left by its citizens. The budget presented in the British Parliament the other day proposes to increase the death-duties; and, most significant of all, the new tax is to be a graduated one. Of all forms of taxation, this seems the wisest. Men who continue hoarding great sums all their lives, the proper use of which for public ends would work good to the community, should be made to feel that the community, in the form of the state, cannot thus be deprived of its proper share. By taxing estates heavily at death the state marks its condemnation of the selfish millionaire's unworthy life.

It is desirable that nations should go much further in this direction. Indeed, it is difficult to set bounds to the share of a rich man's estate which should go at his death to the public through the agency of the state, and by all means such taxes should be graduated, beginning at nothing upon moderate sums to dependents, and increasing rapidly as the amounts swell, until of the millionaire's hoard, as of Shylock's, at least

> —The other half
> Comes to the privy coffer of the state.

This policy would work powerfully to induce the rich man to attend to the administration of wealth during his life, which is the end that society should always have in view, as being that by far most fruitful for the people. Nor need it be feared that this policy would sap the root of enterprise and render men less anxious to accumulate, for to the class whose ambition it is to leave great fortunes and be talked about after their death, it will attract even more attention, and, indeed, be a somewhat nobler ambition to have enormous sums paid over to the state from their fortunes.

There remains, then, only one mode of using great fortunes; but in this we have the true antidote for the temporary unequal distribution of wealth, the reconciliation of the rich and the poor—a reign of harmony—another ideal, differing, indeed, from that of the Communist in requiring only the further evolution of existing conditions, not the total overthrow of our civilization. It is founded upon the present most intense individualism, and the race is prepared to put it in practice by degrees whenever it pleases. Under its sway we shall have an ideal state, in which the surplus wealth of the few will become, in the best sense, the property of the many, because administered for the common good, and this wealth, passing through the hands of the few, can be made a much more potent force for the elevation of our race than if it had been distributed in small sums to the people themselves. Even the poorest can be made to see this, and to agree that great sums gathered by some of their fellow-citizens and spent for public purposes, from which the masses reap the principal benefit, are more valuable to them than if scattered among them through the course of many years in trifling amounts.

If we consider what results flow from the Cooper Institute, for instance, to the best portion of the race in New York not possessed of means, and compare these with those which would have arisen for the good of the masses from an equal sum distributed by Mr. Cooper in his lifetime in the form of wages, which is the highest form of distribution, being for work done and not for charity, we can form some estimate of the possibilities for the improvement of the race which lie embedded in the present law of the accumulation of wealth. Much of this sum, if distributed in small quantities among the people, would have been wasted in the indulgence of appetite, some of it in excess, and it may be doubted whether even the part put to the best use, that of adding to the comforts of the home, would have yielded results for the race, as a race, at all comparable to those which are flowing and are to flow from the Cooper Institute from generation to generation. Let the advocate of violent or radical change ponder well this thought.

We might even go so far as to take another instance, that of Mr. Tilden's bequest of five millions of dollars for a free library in the city of New York, but in referring to this one cannot help saying involuntarily, How much better if Mr. Tilden had devoted the last years of his own life to the proper administration of this immense sum; in which case neither legal contest nor any other cause of delay could have interfered with his aims. But let us assume that Mr. Tilden's millions finally become the means of giving to New York a noble public library, where the treasures of the world contained in books will be open to all forever, without money and without price. Considering the good of that part of the race which congregates in and around Manhattan Island, would its permanent benefit have been better promoted had these millions been allowed to circulate in small sums through the hands of the masses? Even the most strenuous advocate of Communism must entertain a doubt upon this subject. Most of those who think will probably entertain no doubt whatever.

Poor and restricted are our opportunities in this life; narrow our horizon; our best work most imperfect; but rich men should be thankful for one inestimable boon. They have it in their power during their lives to busy themselves in organizing benefactions from which the masses of their fellows will derive lasting advantage, and thus dignify their own lives. The highest life is probably to be reached, not by such imitation of the life of Christ as Count Tolstoi gives us, but, while animated by Christ's spirit, by recognizing the changed conditions of this age, and adopting modes of expressing this spirit suitable to the changed conditions under which we live; still laboring for the good of our fellows, which was the essence of his life and teaching, but laboring in a different manner.

This, then, is held to be the duty of the man of Wealth: First, to set an example of modest, unostentatious living, shunning display or extravagance; to provide moderately for the legitimate wants of those dependent upon him; and after doing so to consider all surplus revenues which come to him simply as trust funds, which he is called upon to administer, and strictly bound as a matter of duty to administer in the manner which, in his judgment, is best calculated to produce the most beneficial results for the community—the man of wealth thus becoming the mere agent and trustee for his poorer brethren, bringing to their service his superior wisdom, experience, and ability to administer, doing for them better than they would or could do for themselves.

We are met here with the difficulty of determining what are moderate sums to leave to members of the family; what is modest, unostentatious living; what is the test of extravagance. There must be different standards for different conditions. The answer is that it is as impossible to name exact amounts or actions as it is to define good manners, good taste, or the rules of propriety; but, nevertheless, these are verities, well known although undefinable. Public sentiment is quick to know and to feel what offends these. So in the case of wealth. The rule in regard to good taste in the dress of men or women applies here. Whatever makes one conspicuous offends the canon. If any family be chiefly known for display, for extravagance in home, table, equipage, for enormous sums ostentatiously spent in any form upon itself,—if these be its chief distinctions, we have no difficulty in estimating its nature or culture. So likewise in regard to the use or abuse of its surplus wealth, or to generous, free-handed cooperation in good public uses, or to unabated efforts to accumulate and hoard to the last, whether they administer or bequeath. The verdict rests with the best and most enlightened public sentiment. The community will surely judge, and its judgments will not often be wrong.

The best uses to which surplus wealth can be put have already been indicated. Those who would administer wisely must, indeed, be wise, for one of the serious obstacles to the improvement of our race is indiscriminate charity. It were better for mankind that the millions of the rich were thrown into the sea than so spent as to encourage the slothful, the drunken, the unworthy. Of every thousand dollars spent in so-called charity to-day, it is probable that $950 is unwisely spent; so spent, indeed, as to produce the very evils which it proposes to mitigate or cure. A well-known writer of philosophic books admitted the other day that he had given a quarter of a dollar to a man who approached him as he was coming to visit the house of his friend. He knew nothing of the habits of this beggar; knew not the use that would be made of this money, although he had every reason to suspect that it would be spent improperly. This man professed to be a disciple of Herbert Spencer; yet the quarter-dollar given that night will probably work more injury than all the money which its thoughtless donor will ever be able to give in true charity will do good. He only gratified his own feelings, saved himself from annoyance,—and this was probably one of the most selfish and very worst actions of his life, for in all respects he is most worthy.

In bestowing charity, the main consideration should be to help those who will help themselves; to provide part of the means by which those who desire to improve may do so; to give those who desire to rise the aids by which they may rise; to assist, but rarely or never to do all. Neither the individual nor the race is improved by alms-giving. Those worthy of assistance, except in rare cases, seldom require assistance. The really valuable men of the race never do, except in cases of accident or sudden change. Every one has, of course, cases of individuals brought to his own knowledge where temporary assistance can do genuine good, and these he will not overlook. But the amount which can be wisely given by the individual for individuals is necessarily limited by his lack of knowledge of the circumstances connected with each. He is the only true reformer who is as careful and as anxious not to aid the unworthy as he is to aid the worthy, and, perhaps, even more so, for in alms-giving more injury is probably done by rewarding vice than by relieving virtue.

The rich man is thus almost restricted to following the examples of Peter Cooper, Enoch Pratt of Baltimore, Mr. Pratt of Brooklyn, Senator Stanford, and others, who know that the best means of benefiting the community is to place within its reach the ladders upon which the aspiring can rise—parks, and means of recreation, by which men are helped in body and mind; works of art, certain to give pleasure and improve the public taste; and public institutions of various kinds, which will improve the general condition of the people;—in this manner returning their surplus wealth to the mass of their fellows in the forms best calculated to do them lasting good.

Thus is the problem of Rich and Poor to be solved. The laws of accumulation will be left free; the laws of distribution free. Individualism will continue, but the millionaire will be but a trustee for the poor; intrusted for a season with a great part of the increased wealth of the community, but administering it for the community far better than it could or would have done for itself. The best minds will thus have reached a stage in the development of the race in which it is clearly seen that there is no mode of disposing of surplus wealth creditable to thoughtful and earnest men into whose hands it flows save by using it year by year for the general good. This day already dawns. But a little while, and although, without incurring the pity of their fellows, men may die sharers in great business enterprises from which their capital cannot be or has not been withdrawn, and is left chiefly at death for public uses, yet the man who dies leaving behind him millions of available wealth, which was his to administer during life, will pass away "unwept, unhonored, and unsung," no matter to what uses he leaves the dross which he cannot take with him. Of such as these the public verdict will then be: "The man who dies thus rich dies disgraced."

Such, in my opinion, is the true Gospel concerning Wealth, obedience to which is destined some day to solve the problem of the Rich and the Poor, and to bring "Peace on earth, among men Good-Will."

THE BEST FIELDS FOR PHILANTHROPY

The reception given to the first paper upon this subject, to which our lamented friend, the late editor and proprietor of this *Review*, was pleased to give the first place in the June number, has been most encouraging to its author, as it would surely have been to the editor had he been spared, for he was most deeply interested in the subject. As showing the unflagging attention which Mr. Rice bestowed upon his editorial duties, it may be permissible to tell that the manuscript reached him in the morning, and late in the evening of the same day he called to say that it pleased him so much that he had determined to publish it in the forthcoming number, instead of holding it for the succeeding issue, as had been intended. When urged to delay publication, that proper time might be given for revision, he declined. Had he complied, another than he, alas! would have had to stand sponsor for my thoughts. Only one short week, and our friend was at rest; his warfare o'er. He had played his part in life well; and yet how little is he, or is any one, missed upon the march! The race presses slowly on as before; another rises to take the vacant place; the *North American Review* shines on, a lamp still burning, to show the great army of humanity the pitfalls which it must avoid in order to retain what has been already conquered, and to light the paths which that army must tread on its way to future conquests. In the death of Mr. Rice we have another proof that in the progress of humanity persons are little or nothing; the race is all.

The individual withers, and the world is more and more.

And yet it is much to me that probably the last manuscript our friend read, valued, and published was "Wealth." Perhaps your readers will pardon me for recalling an incident connected with our last interview. Sitting in my library, Mr. Rice expressed a wish to hear the author read his manuscript. I read and he listened from beginning to end, making but one interruption. When the passage was read which stated that, of every thousand dollars spent to-day in so-called charity, probably nine hundred was unwisely spent, he exclaimed, "Yes, nine hundred and fifty! Make it nine hundred and fifty!" and it was so made. I cannot pass without paying a tribute to Allen Thorndike Rice. That I knew him is one of the sources from which sweet remembrances spring at times, when free from the roar and bustle of life.

While "Wealth" has thus met a cordial reception upon this side of the Atlantic, it is natural that in the mother-land it should have attracted most attention, because the older civilization is at present brought more clearly face to face with socialistic questions. The contrast between the classes and the masses, between rich and poor, is not yet quite so sharp in this vast, fertile, and developing continent, with less than twenty persons per square mile, as in crowded little Britain, with fifteen times that number and no territory unoccupied. Perhaps the *Pall Mall Gazette* in its issue of September 5 puts most pithily the objections that have been raised to what the English have been pleased to call the "Gospel of Wealth." It says:

Great fortunes, says Mr. Carnegie, are great blessings to a community, because such and such things may be done with them. Well, but they are also a great curse, for such and such things are done with them. Mr. Carnegie's preaching, in other words, is altogether vitiated by Mr. Benzon's practice. The "Gospel of Wealth" is killed by the acts.

To this the reply seems obvious: the gospel of Christianity is also killed by the acts. The same objection that is urged against the gospel of wealth lies against the commandment "Thou shalt not steal." It is no argument against a gospel that it is not lived up to; indeed, it is an argument in its favor, for a gospel must be higher than the prevailing standard. It is no argument against a law that it is broken: in that disobedience lies the reason for making and maintaining the law; the law which is never to be broken is never required.

Undoubtedly the most notable incident in regard to the "Gospel of Wealth" is that it was fortunate enough to attract the attention of Mr. Gladstone, and brought forth the following note from him:

I have asked Mr. Lloyd Bryce (*North American Review*) kindly to allow the republication in this country of the extremely interesting article on

"Wealth," by Mr. Andrew Carnegie, which has just appeared in America.

This resulted in the publication of the article in several newspapers and periodicals, and an enterprising publisher issued it in pamphlet form. It is now sold in Britain for a penny.

All this is most encouraging, proving, as it does, that society is alive to the great issue involved, and is in a receptive mood. Your request, Mr. Editor, that I should continue the subject and point out the best fields for the use of surplus wealth may be taken as further proof that whether the ideas promulgated are to be received or rejected, they are at least certain to obtain a hearing.

Before entering upon the question which you have proposed, it may be advantageous to restate the positions taken in the former paper, for the benefit of those who may not have read it, or who cannot conveniently refer to it. It was assumed that the present laws of competition, accumulation, and distribution are the best obtainable conditions; that through these the race receives its most valuable fruits; and, therefore, that they should be accepted and upheld. Under these it was held that great wealth must inevitably flow into the hands of the few exceptional managers of men. The question then arose, What should these do with their surplus wealth? and the "Gospel of Wealth" contended that surplus wealth should be considered as a sacred trust, to be administered during the lives of its owners, by them as trustees, for the best good of the community in which and from which it had been acquired.

It was pointed out that there were but three modes of disposing of surplus wealth, and two of these were held to be improper.

First, it was held that to leave great fortunes to children did not prove true affection for them or interest in their genuine good, regarded either as individuals or as members of the state; that it was not the welfare of the children, but the pride of the parents, which inspired enormous legacies, and that, looking to the usual results of vast sums conferred upon children, the thoughtful man must be forced to say, if the good of the child only were considered: "I would as soon leave to my son a curse as to leave to him the almighty dollar."

The second mode open to men is to hoard their surplus wealth during life, and leave it at death for public uses. It was pointed out that in many cases these bequests become merely monuments of the testators' folly; that the amount of real good done by posthumous gifts was ridiculously disproportionate to the sums thus left. The recent decision upon Mr. Tilden's will, which is said to have been drawn by the ablest of lawyers, and the partial failure of Mr. Williamson's purposes in regard to the great technical school which that millionaire intended to establish in Philadelphia, are lessons indeed for the rich who only bequeath.

The aim of the first article was thus to lead up to the conclusion that there is but one right mode of using enormous fortunes—namely, that the possessors from time to time during their own lives should so administer them as to promote the permanent good of the communities from which they have been gathered. It was held that public sentiment would soon say of one who died possessed of millions of available wealth which he might have administered: "The man who dies thus rich dies disgraced."

The purpose of this article is to present some of the best methods of performing this duty of administering surplus wealth for the good of the people. The first requisite for a really good use of wealth by the millionaire who has accepted the gospel which proclaims him only a trustee of the surplus that comes to him is to take care that the purpose for which he spends it shall not have a degrading, pauperizing tendency upon its recipients, and that his trust should be so administered as to stimulate the best and most aspiring poor of the community to further efforts for their own improvement. It is not the irreclaimably destitute, shiftless, and worthless that it is truly beneficial or truly benevolent to attempt to reach and improve. For these there exists the refuge provided by the city or the state, where they can be sheltered, fed, clothed, and kept in comfortable existence, and—most important of all—where they can be isolated from the well-doing and industrious poor, who are liable to be demoralized by contact with these unfortunates. One man or woman who succeeds in living comfortably by begging is more dangerous to society, and a greater obstacle to the progress of humanity, than a score of wordy Socialists. The individual administrator of surplus wealth has as his charge the industrious and ambitious; not those who need everything done for them, but those who, being most anxious and able to help themselves, deserve and will be benefited by help from others and the extension of their opportunities at the hands of the philanthropic rich.

It is ever to be remembered that one of the chief obstacles which the philanthropist meets in his efforts to do real and permanent good in this world is the practice of indiscriminate giving; and the duty of the millionaire is to resolve to cease giving to objects that are not proved clearly to his satisfaction to be deserving. He must remember Mr. Rice's belief that nine hundred and fifty out of every thousand dollars bestowed to-day upon so-called charity had better be thrown into the sea. As far as my experience of the wealthy extends, it is unnecessary to urge them to give of their superabundance in charity so-called. Greater good for the race is to be achieved by inducing them to cease impulsive and injurious giving. As a rule, the sins of millionaires in this respect are not those of omission, but of commission, because they will not take time to think, and chiefly because it is much easier to give than to refuse. Those who have surplus wealth give millions every year which produce more evil than good, and which really retard the progress of the people, because most of the forms in vogue to-day for benefiting mankind only tend to spread among the poor a spirit of dependence upon alms, when what is essential for progress is that they should be inspired to depend upon their own exertions. The miser millionaire who hoards his wealth does less injury to society than the careless millionaire who squanders his unwisely, even if he does so under cover of the mantle of sacred charity. The man who gives to the individual beggar commits a grave offence, but there are many societies and institutions soliciting alms which it is none the less injurious to the community to aid. These are as corrupting as individual beggars. Plutarch's "Morals" contains this lesson: "A beggar asking an alms of a Lacedæmonian, he said: 'Well, should I give thee anything, thou wilt be the greater beggar, for he that first gave thee money made thee idle, and is the cause of this base and dishonorable way of living.' " As I know them, there are few millionaires, very few indeed, who are clear of this sin of having made beggars.

Bearing in mind these considerations, let us endeavor to present some of the best uses to which a millionaire can devote the surplus of which he should regard himself as only the trustee.

First—Standing apart by itself there is the founding of a university by men enormously rich, such men as must necessarily be few in any country. Perhaps the greatest sum ever given by an individual for any purpose is the gift of Senator Stanford, who undertakes to establish upon the Pacific coast, where he amassed his enormous fortune, a complete university, which is said to involve the expenditure of ten millions of dollars, and upon which he may be expected to bestow twenty millions of his surplus. He is to be envied. A thousand years hence some orator, speaking his praise upon the then crowded shores of the Pacific, may repeat Griffith's eulogy of Wolsey, "In bestowing he was most princely: ever witness for him this great seat of learning." Here is a noble use of wealth.

We have many such institutions, Hopkins, Cornell, Packer, and others, but most of these have only been bequeathed, and it is impossible to extol any man greatly for simply leaving what he cannot take with him. Cooper, and Pratt, and Stanford, and others of this class deserve credit and the admiration of their fellows as much for the time and the attention given during their lives, as for their expenditure, upon their respective monuments.

We cannot have the Pacific coast in mind without recalling another important work of a different character which has recently been established there, the Lick Observatory. If any millionaire be interested in the ennobling study of astronomy,—and there should be and would be such if they but gave the subject the slightest attention,—here is an example which could well be followed, for the progress made in astronomical instruments and appliances is so great and continuous that every few years a new telescope might be judiciously given to one of the observatories upon this continent, the last being always the largest and the best, and certain to carry further and further the knowledge of the universe and of our relation to it here upon the earth. As one among many of the good deeds of the late Mr. Thaw, of Pittsburg, his constant support of the observatory there may be mentioned. This observatory enabled Professor Langley to make his wonderful discoveries. The professor is now at the head of the Smithsonian Institution, a worthy successor to Professor Henry. Connected with him was Mr.

Braeshier, of Pittsburg, whose instruments are in most of the principal observatories of the world. He was a common millwright, but Mr. Thaw recognized his genius and was his main support through trying days. This common workman has been made a professor by one of the foremost scientific bodies of the world. In applying part of his surplus in aiding these two now famous men, the millionaire Thaw did a noble work. Their joint labors have brought great, and are destined to bring still greater, credit upon their country in every scientific centre throughout the world.

It is reserved for very few to found universities, and, indeed, the use for many, or perhaps any, new universities does not exist. More good is henceforth to be accomplished by adding to and extending those in existence. But in this department a wide field remains for the millionaire as distinguished from the Crœsus among millionaires. The gifts to Yale University have been many, but there is plenty of room for others. The School of Fine Arts, founded by Mr. Street, the Sheffield Scientific School, endowed by Mr. Sheffield, and Professor Loomis's fund for the observatory, are fine examples. Mrs. C. J. Osborne's building for reading and recitation is to be regarded with especial pleasure as being the wise gift of a woman. Harvard University has not been forgotten; the Peabody Museum, and the halls of Wells, Matthews, and Thayer may be cited. Seber Hall is worthy of special mention, as showing what a genius like Richardson could do with the small sum of a hundred thousand dollars. The Vanderbilt University at Nashville, Tennessee, may be mentioned as a true product of the gospel of wealth. It was established by members of the Vanderbilt family during their lives—mark this vital feature—during their lives; for nothing counts for much that is left by a man at his death. Such funds are torn from him, not given by him. If any millionaire is at a loss to know how to accomplish great and indisputable good with his surplus, here is a field which can never be fully occupied, for the wants of our universities increase with the development of the country.

Second—The result of my own study of the question, What is the best gift which can be given to a community? is that a free library occupies the first place, provided the community will accept and maintain it as a public institution, as much a part of the city property as its public schools, and, indeed, an adjunct to these. It is, no doubt, possible that my own personal experience may have led me to value a free library beyond all other forms of beneficence. When I was a boy in Pittsburg, Colonel Anderson, of Allegheny,—a name I can never speak without feelings of devotional gratitude,—opened his little library of four hundred books to boys. Every Saturday afternoon he was in attendance himself at his house to exchange books. No one but he who has felt it can know the intense longing with which the arrival of Saturday was awaited, that a new book might be had. My brother and Mr. Phipps, who have been my principal business partners through life, shared with me Colonel Anderson's precious generosity, and it was when revelling in these treasures that I resolved, if ever wealth came to me, that it should be used to establish free libraries, that other poor boys might receive opportunities similar to those for which we were indebted to that noble man.

Great Britain has been foremost in appreciating the value of free libraries for its people. Parliament passed an act permitting towns and cities to establish and maintain these as municipal institutions, and whenever the people of any town or city voted to accept the provisions of the act, the authorities were authorized to tax the community to the extent of one penny in the pound valuation. Most of the towns already have free libraries under this act. Many of these are the gifts of rich men, whose funds have been used for the building, and in some cases for the books also, the communities being required to maintain and to develop the libraries; and to this feature I attribute most of their usefulness. An endowed institution is liable to become the prey of a clique. The public ceases to take interest in it, or, rather, never acquires interest in it. The rule has been violated which requires the recipients to help themselves. Everything has been done for the community instead of its being only helped to help itself.

Many free libraries have been established in our country, but none that I know of with such wisdom as the Pratt Library, of Baltimore. Mr. Pratt presented to the city of Baltimore one million dollars, requiring it to pay 5 per cent per annum, amounting to fifty thousand dollars per year, which is to be devoted to the maintenance and development of the library and its branches. During last year 430,217 books were distributed; 37,196 people of Baltimore are registered upon the books as readers; and it is safe to say that the 37,000 frequenters of the Pratt Library are of more value to

Baltimore, to the State, and to the country than all the inert, lazy, and hopelessly-poor in the whole nation. And it may further be safely said that, by placing within the reach of 37,000 aspiring people books which they were anxious to obtain, Mr. Pratt has done more for the genuine progress of the people than has been done by all the contributions of all the millionaires and rich people to help those who cannot help themselves. The one wise administrator of his surplus has poured his fertilizing stream upon soil that was ready to receive it and return a hundred-fold. The many squanderers have not only poured their streams into sieves which never can be filled,— they have done worse; they have poured them into stagnant sewers that breed the diseases which afflict the body politic. And this is not all. The million dollars of which Mr. Pratt has made so grand a use are something, but there is something greater still. When the fifth branch library was opened in Baltimore, the speaker said:

Whatever may have been done in these four years, it was his pleasure to acknowledge that much, very much, was due to the earnest interest, the wise councils, and the practical suggestions of Mr. Pratt. He never seemed to feel that the mere donation of great wealth for the benefit of his fellow-citizens was all that would be asked of him, but he wisely labored to make its application as comprehensive and effective as possible. Thus he constantly lightened burdens that were, at times, very heavy, brought good cheer and bright sunshine when clouds flitted across the sky, and made every officer and employee feel that good work was appreciated, and loyal devotion to duty would receive hearty commendation.

This is the finest picture I have ever seen of any of the millionaire class. As here depicted, Mr. Pratt is the ideal disciple of the "Gospel of Wealth." We need have no fear that the mass of toilers will fail to recognize in such as he their best leaders and their most invaluable allies; for the problem of poverty and wealth, of employer and employed, will be practically solved whenever the time of the few is given, and their wealth is administered during their lives, for the best good of that portion of the community which has not been burdened by the responsibilities which attend the possession of wealth. We shall have no antagonism between classes when that day comes, for the high and the low, the rich and the poor, shall then indeed be brothers.

No millionaire will go far wrong in his search for one of the best forms for the use of his surplus who chooses to establish a free library in any community that is willing to maintain and develop it. John Bright's words should ring in his ear: "It is impossible for any man to bestow a greater benefit upon a young man than to give him access to books in a free library." Closely allied to the library, and, where possible, attached to it, there should be rooms for an art gallery and museum, and a hall for such lectures and instruction as are provided in the Cooper Union. The traveller upon the Continent is surprised to find that every town of importance has its art gallery and museum; these may be large or small, but in any case each has a receptacle for the treasures of the locality, which is constantly receiving valuable gifts and bequests. The free library and art gallery of Birmingham are remarkable among these, and every now and then a rich man adds to their value by presenting books, fine pictures, or other works of art. All that our cities require to begin with is a proper fire-proof building. Their citizens who travel will send to it rare and costly things from every quarter of the globe they visit, while those who remain at home will give or bequeath to it of their treasures. In this way these collections will grow until our cities will ultimately be able to boast of permanent exhibitions from which their own citizens will derive incalculable benefit, and which they will be proud to show to visitors. In the Metropolitan Museum of Art in this city we have made an excellent beginning. Here is another avenue for the proper use of surplus wealth.

Third—We have another most important department in which great sums can be worthily used,—the founding or extension of hospitals, medical colleges, laboratories, and other institutions connected with the alleviation of human suffering, and especially with the prevention rather than the cure of human ills. There is no danger of pauperizing a community in giving for such purposes, because such institutions relieve temporary ailments or shelter only those who are hopeless invalids. What better gift than a hospital can be given to a community that is without one?—the gift being conditioned upon its proper maintenance by the community in its corporate capacity. If hospital accommodation already exists, no better method for using surplus wealth can be found than in making additions to it. The late Mr. Vanderbilt's gift of half a million of dollars to the medical department of Columbia College for a chemical laboratory was one of the wisest possible uses of wealth. It strikes at the prevention of disease by penetrating into its causes. Several others have established such laboratories, but the need for them is still great.

If there be a millionaire in the land who is at a loss what to do with the surplus that has been committed to him as trustee, let him investigate the good that is flowing from these chemical laboratories. No medical college is complete without its laboratory. As with universities, so with medical colleges; it is not new institutions that are required, but additional means for the more thorough equipment of those that exist. The forms that benefactions to these may wisely take are numerous, but probably none is more useful than that adopted by Mr. Osborne when he built a school for training female nurses at Bellevue College. If from all gifts there flows one-half of the good that comes from this wise use of a millionaire's surplus, the most exacting may well be satisfied. Only those who have passed through a lingering and dangerous illness can rate at their true value the care, skill, and attendance of trained female nurses. Their employment as nurses has enlarged the sphere and influence of woman. It is not to be wondered at that a Senator of the United States and a physician distinguished in this country for having received the highest distinctions abroad should find their wives from this class.

Fourth—In the very front rank of benefactions public parks should be placed, always provided that the community undertakes to maintain, beautify, and preserve inviolate the parks given to it. No more useful or more beautiful monument can be left by any man than a park for the city in which he was born or in which he has long lived, nor can the community pay a more graceful tribute to the citizen who presents it than to give his name to the gift. If a park be already provided, there is still room for many judicious gifts in connection with it. Mr. Phipps, of Allegheny, has given conservatories to the park there, which are visited by many every day of the week and crowded by thousands of working people every Sunday, for, with rare wisdom, he has stipulated as a condition of the gift that the conservatories shall be open on Sundays. The result of his experiment has been so gratifying that he is justified in adding to them from his surplus, as he is doing largely this year. To any lover of flowers among the wealthy I commend a study of what is possible for them to do in the line of Mr. Phipps's example; and may they please note that Mr. Phipps is a wise as well as a liberal giver, for he requires the city to maintain these conservatories, and thus secures for them forever the public ownership, the public interest, and the public criticism of their management. Had he undertaken to manage and maintain them, it is probable that popular interest in the gift would never have been awakened.

The parks and pleasure-grounds of small towns throughout Europe are not less surprising than their libraries, museums, and art galleries. We saw nothing more pleasing during our recent travels than the hillside of Bergen, in Norway. It has been converted into one of the most picturesque of pleasure-grounds; fountains, cascades, water-falls, delightful arbors, fine terraces, and statues adorn what was before a barren mountain side. Here is a field worthy of study by the millionaire who would confer a lasting benefit upon his fellows. Another beautiful instance of the right use of wealth in the direction of making cities more and more attractive we found in Dresden. The owner of the leading paper there bequeathed its revenues forever to the city, to be used in beautifying it. An art committee decides from time to time what new artistic feature is to be introduced or what hideous feature is to be changed, and as the revenues accrue they are expended in this direction. Thus through the gift of this patriotic newspaper proprietor his native city of Dresden is fast becoming one of the most artistic places of residence in the whole world. A work having been completed, it devolves upon the city to maintain it forever. May I be excused if I commend to our millionaire newspaper proprietors the example of their colleague in the capital of Saxony?

Scarcely a city of any magnitude in the older countries is without many structures and features of great beauty. Much has been spent upon ornament, decoration, and architectural effect: we are still far behind in these things upon this side of the Atlantic. Our Republic is great in some things,—in material development unrivalled; but let us always remember that in art and in the finer touches we have scarcely yet taken a place. Had the exquisite memorial arch recently erected temporarily in New York been shown in Dresden, the art committee there would probably have been enabled, from the revenue of the newspaper given by its owner for just such purposes, to order its permanent erection to adorn the city forever.

While the bestowal of a park upon a community as one of the best uses for surplus wealth will be universally approved, in embracing such additions to it as conservatories, or in advocating the building of memorial arches and works of adornment, it is probable that many will think we go too far, and consider these somewhat fanciful. The material good to flow from them may not be so directly visible; but let not any practical mind, intent only upon material good, depreciate the value of wealth given for these or for kindred æsthetic purposes as being useless as far as the mass of the people and their needs are concerned. As with libraries and museums, so with these more distinctively artistic works; these perform their great use when they reach the best of the masses of the people. It is worth more to reach and touch the sentiment for beauty in the naturally bright minds of this class than that those incapable of being so touched should be pandered to. For what the improver of the race must endeavor to do is to reach those who have the divine spark ever so feebly developed, that it may be strengthened and grow. For my part, I think Mr. Phipps put his money to better use in giving the workingmen of Allegheny conservatories filled with beautiful flowers, orchids, and aquatic plants, which they, with their wives and children, can enjoy in their spare hours, and on which they can feed the love for the beautiful, than if he had given his surplus money to furnish them with bread, for those in health who cannot earn their bread are scarcely worth considering by the individual giver; the care of such being the duty of the state. The man who erects in a city a truly artistic arch, statue, or fountain makes a wise use of his surplus. "Man does not live by bread alone."

Fifth—We have another good use for surplus wealth, in providing for our cities halls suitable for meetings of all kinds, especially for concerts of elevating music. Our cities are rarely provided with halls for these purposes, being in this respect also very far behind European cities. The Springer Hall, of Cincinnati, that valuable addition to the city, was largely the gift of Mr. Springer, who was not content to bequeath funds from his estate at death, but who gave during his life, and, in addition, gave—what was equally important—his time and business ability to insure the successful results which have been achieved. The gift of a hall to any city lacking one is an excellent use for surplus wealth for the good of a community. The reason why the people have only one instructive and elevating, or even amusing, entertainment when a dozen would be highly beneficial is that the rent of a hall, even when a suitable hall exists (which is rare), is so great as to prevent managers from running the risk of financial failure. If every city in our land owned a hall which could be given or rented for a small sum for such gatherings as a committee or the mayor of the city judged advantageous, the people could be furnished with proper lectures, amusements, and concerts at an exceedingly small cost. The town halls of European cities, many of which have organs, are of inestimable value to the people, when utilized as they are in the manner suggested. Let no one underrate the influence of entertainments of an elevating or even of an amusing character, for these do much to make the lives of the people happier and their natures better. If any millionaire born in a small village, which has now become a great city, is prompted in the day of his success to do something for his birth-place with part of his surplus, his grateful remembrance cannot take a form more useful than that of a public hall with an organ, provided the city agrees to maintain and use it.

Sixth—In another respect we are still much behind Europe. A form of beneficence which is not uncommon there is providing swimming baths for the people. The donors of these have been wise enough to require the city benefited to maintain them at its own expense, and as proof of the contention that everything should never be done for any one or for any community, but that the recipients should invariably be called upon to do part, it is significant that it is found essential for the popular success of these healthful establishments to exact a nominal charge for their use. In many cities, however, the school children are admitted free at fixed hours upon certain days, different hours being fixed for the boys and the girls to use the great swimming baths, hours or days being also fixed for the use of these baths by ladies. In inland cities the young of both sexes are thus taught to swim. Swimming clubs are organized, and matches are frequent, at which medals and prizes are given. The reports published by the various swimming baths throughout Great Britain are filled with instances of lives saved because those who fortunately escaped shipwreck had been taught to swim in the baths, and not a few instances are given in which the pupils of certain bathing establishments have saved the lives of others. If any disciple of the "Gospel of Wealth" gives his favorite city large swimming and private baths (provided the municipality undertakes their management as a city affair), he will never be called to account for an improper use of the funds intrusted to him.

Seventh—Churches as fields for the use of surplus wealth have purposely been reserved until the last, because, these being sectarian, every man will be governed by his own attachments; therefore gifts to churches, it may be said, are not, in one sense, gifts to the community at large, but to special classes. Nevertheless, every millionaire may know of a district where the little cheap, uncomfortable, and altogether unworthy wooden structure stands at the crossroads, to which the whole neighborhood gathers on Sunday, and which is the centre of social life and source of neighborly feeling. The administrator of wealth has made a good use of part of his surplus if he replaces that building with a permanent structure of brick, stone, or granite, up the sides of which the honeysuckle and columbine may climb, and from whose tower the sweet-tolling bell may sound. The millionaire should not figure how cheaply this structure can be built, but how perfect it can be made. If he has the money, it should be made a gem, for the educating influence of a pure and noble specimen of architecture, built, as the pyramids were built, to stand for ages, is not to be measured by dollars. Every farmer's home, heart, and mind in the district will be influenced by the beauty and grandeur of the church. But having given the building, the donor should stop there; the support of the church should be upon its own people; there is not much genuine religion in the congregation or much good to flow from the church which is not supported at home.

Many other avenues for the wise expenditure of surplus wealth might be indicated. I enumerate but a few—a very few—of the many fields which are open, and only those in which great or considerable sums can be judiciously used. It is not the privilege, however, of millionaires alone to work for or aid measures which are certain to benefit the community. Every one who has but a small surplus above his moderate wants may share this privilege with his richer brothers, and those without surplus can give at least part of their time, which is usually as important as funds, and often more so. Some day, perhaps, with your permission, I will endeavor to point out some fields and modes in which these may perform well their part as trustees of wealth or leisure, according to the measure of their respective fortunes.

It is not expected, neither is it desirable, that there should be a general concurrence as to the best possible use of surplus wealth. For different men and different localities there are different uses. What commends itself most highly to the judgment of the administrator is the best use for him, for his heart should be in the work. It is as important in administering wealth as it is in any other branch of a man's work that he should be enthusiastically devoted to it and feel that in the field selected his work lies.

Besides this, there is room and need for all kinds of wise benefactions for the common weal. The man who builds a university, library, or laboratory performs no more useful work than he who elects to devote himself and his surplus means to the adornment of a park, the gathering together of a collection of pictures for the public, or the building of a memorial arch. These are all true laborers in the vineyard. The only point required by the "Gospel of Wealth" is that the surplus which accrues from time to time in the hands of a man should be administered by him in his own lifetime for that purpose which is seen by him, as trustee, to be best for the good of the people. To leave at death what he cannot take away, and place upon others the burden of the work which it was his own duty to perform, is to do nothing worthy. This requires no sacrifice, nor any sense of duty to his fellows.

Time was when the words concerning the rich man entering heaven were regarded as a hard saying. To-day, when all questions are probed to the bottom and the standards of faith receive the most liberal interpretations, the startling verse has been relegated to the rear, to await the next kindly revision as one of those things which cannot be quite understood, but which meanwhile—it is carefully to be observed—are not to be understood literally. But is it so very improbable that the next stage of thought is not to restore the doctrine in all its pristine purity and force, as being in perfect harmony with sound ideas upon the subject of wealth and poverty, the rich and the poor, and the contrasts everywhere seen and deplored? In Christ's day, it is evident, reformers were against the wealthy. It is none the less evident that we are fast recurring to that position to-day; and there will be nothing to surprise the student of sociological development if society should soon approve the text which has caused so much anxiety: "It is easier for a camel to enter the eye of a needle than for a rich man to enter the Kingdom of Heaven." Even if the needle were the small casement at the gates, the words betoken serious difficulty for the rich. It will be but a step for the theologian to take from the doctrine that he who dies rich dies disgraced to that which brings upon the man punishment or deprivation hereafter.

The "Gospel of Wealth" but echoes Christ's words. It calls upon the millionaire to sell all that he hath and give it in the highest and best form to the poor, by administering his estate himself for the good of his fellows, before he is called upon to lie down and rest upon the bosom of Mother Earth. So doing, he will approach his end no longer the ignoble hoarder of useless millions, poor, very poor indeed, in money, but rich, very rich, twenty times a millionaire still, in the affection, gratitude, and admiration of his fellow-men, and—sweeter far—soothed and sustained by the still small voice within, which, whispering, tells him that, because he has lived, perhaps one small part of the great world has been bettered just a little. This much is sure: against such riches as these no bar will be found at the Gates of Paradise.

THE ADVANTAGES OF POVERTY

Two essays from my pen, published in the *North American Review* , have been doubly fortunate in Britain in being reprinted by the *Pall Mall Gazette* under the new and striking title of "The Gospel of Wealth,"[1] and in attracting the attention of the one man who, of all others, could bring them most prominently before thinking people. Mr. Gladstone's review and recommendation in the November number of this *Review* gave them the most illustrious of sponsors; he is followed in the December number by others of the highest eminence and authority. The discussion has taken a wide range, but I shall restrict myself to its bearings upon the ideas presented in "The Gospel of Wealth."

Mr. Gladstone first calls attention to the portentous growth of wealth. From every point of view this growth seems to me most beneficial; for we know that, rapid as is its growth, its distribution among the people in streams more and more numerous is still more rapid, the share of the joint product of capital and labour which has gone to labour during this generation being much greater than in any generation preceding, and constantly increasing. Evidences, drawn from many independent sources, converge and prove this beyond question. A few enormous fortunes have been amassed during the present generation in this new and undeveloped continent, but under conditions which no longer exist. In our day, even in the United States, it is much easier to lose a great fortune than to make one, and more are being lost than made. It is rather surprising, therefore, that the Rev. Mr. Hughes should say:—

Whatever may be thought of Mr. Henry George's doctrines and deductions, no one can deny that his facts are indisputable, and that Mr. Carnegie's "progress" is accompanied by the growing "poverty" of his less fortunate fellow-countrymen. (P. 891.)

I do not know a writer of authority upon social and economic subjects who has not only disputed Mr. George's statements, but who has not pronounced their opposites to be the truth. Mr. George's *Progress and Poverty* is founded upon two statements: first, that the rich are growing richer, and the poor poorer; and second, that land is going more and more into the hands of the few. The truth is, that the rich are growing poorer and the poor growing richer, and that the land is passing from the hands of the few into the hands of the many. A study of Mulhall's *Fifty Years of National Progress* (pages 23-27) is strongly recommended to those desirous of learning the truth in regard to the distribution of wealth, upon which Mr. Mulhall says:—

Nor does this wealth become congested among a small number of people; on the contrary, the rich grow less rich and more numerous every year, the poor fewer in ratio to population. (P. 23.)

The same results are shown even in a more remarkable degree in the Republic.

In regard to land, the United States Census gives the number and average size of farms as follows:—

Number of Farms

1850	1860	1870	1880
1,449,073	2,044,077	2,659,985	4,008,907

Average size of Farms

Acres	203	199	153	134

This tendency to more numerous and smaller holdings exists also in Britain, although hampered in its operation by repressive laws.

I rejoice that Mr. Hughes quotes the well-known passage from Herbert Spencer, which, as he says, "exposes the sad delusion that great wealth is a great blessing"—a passage which is throughout profoundly true; but is it possible that Mr. Hughes can be uninformed of the position Mr. George occupies in the wise mind of our mutual teacher? In speaking to Mr.

Spencer of Mr. George's book, Mr. Spencer told me that he had read a few pages, and then thrown it down as "trash." I know of no writer or thinker of recognised authority, except Mr. Hughes, who differs with the philosopher in this judgment.

So far as the reference to myself is concerned—I understand, of course, it is in nowise personal, but only as the representative of a class—I beg to assure Mr. Hughes that the indisputable fact I know is that my "progress" has inevitably carried with it, not "the growing poverty," but inevitably the growing riches of my fellow-countrymen as the progress of every employer of labour must necessarily carry with it the enrichment of the country and of the labourer. Imagine one speaking of "growing poverty" in the United States. The American, more than any other workman, spends his savings for the purchase of a home. The savings banks are only one of several depositories used by him.

Nevertheless, the returns just made for the year 1890, for all the New England and Middle States (where millionaires do most abound), comprising a population of 17,300,000—more than half the total population of Britain—show that the deposits are $1,279,000,000—say 255 millions sterling, the increase for the year being thirteen millions sterling. The number of depositors is 3,520,000, showing that about one out of every five men, women, and children has a bank account, equal practically to one to each family. The amount of savings invested for homes far exceeds the savings-bank deposits.

The United States Census, 1880, shows only 88,665 public paupers in a population of 50,000,000, mainly aged and superannuated—one-third being foreigners. There were more blind and idiotic people in the public charitable institutions than paupers, and half as many deaf mutes, although the percentage of the "defective classes" is less than half that of Europe. The total number of all "dependent" persons cared for was less than five per thousand, as compared with thirty-three per thousand in the United Kingdom. This percentage for Britain is happily only about one-fourth of what it has been, and its steady decrease is most encouraging. Good and charitable workers among the poor can best accelerate this decreasing process, until something like the American figure is reached, by instilling within the working classes of Britain those feelings of manly self-respect and those habits of sobriety and thrift which distinguish their race here, and keep it almost free, not only from pauperism, but from want or extreme poverty, except as the necessary result (accident and sickness excepted) of their own bad habits.

Mr. Hughes would not give currency knowingly to statements that were the reverse of correct. I earnestly hope, therefore, that he will satisfy himself that every writer of authority is not deceived when he asserts that poverty, want, and pauperism are rapidly diminishing quantities; and most significantly so, not so much through alms-giving, or efforts of the rich, but because of an improvement through education in the habits of the people themselves—the only foundation upon which their continued progress can surely be built. Mr. Hughes can also readily learn another indisputable fact by inquiring at the shipyards of Glasgow, the iron and steel mills of Sheffield, the coal mines of the Midlands, or at industrial establishments generally, viz. that the working classes receive much greater compensation for their services than they ever did, or now do for any other form of labour, and much greater than they could possibly receive, except for the establishment of great enterprises by men of wealth. In these days of excitement and exaggeration, let it always be borne in mind that at no period in the history of the English-speaking race, wherever that race resides, has it been so easy as it is to-day for the masses, not only to earn comfortable livelihoods, but to save and have money in bank for a rainy day. When they fail to do so, the true reformer looks more to their habits than to existing conditions for a satisfactory explanation.

So far from it being a fact that "millionaires at one end of the scale mean paupers at the other," as Mr. Hughes says, the reverse is obviously true. In a country where the millionaire exists there is little excuse for pauperism; the condition of the masses is satisfactory just in proportion as a country is blessed with millionaires. There is not a millionaire among the whole four hundred millions of China, nor one in Japan, nor in India, one or two perhaps in the whole of Russia, there are two or three in Germany, and not more than four or five in the whole of France, monarchs and hereditary nobles excepted. There are more millionaires upon the favoured little isle of Britain than in the whole of Europe, and in the United States still more, of recent origin, than in Britain; and the revenues of the masses are just in proportion to the ease with which millionaires grow. The British labourer receives more for one day's handling of the shovel than the blacksmith or carpenter of China, Russia, India, and Japan receives for a whole week's labour, and double that of his Continental fellow-workman. The skilled artisan of America receives more than double the artisan of Britain. Millionaires can only grow amidst general prosperity, and this very prosperity is largely promoted by their exertions. Their wealth is not made, as Mr. Hughes implies, at the expense of their fellow-countrymen. Millionaires make no money when compelled to pay low wages. Their profits accrue in periods when wages are high, and the higher the wages that have to be paid, the higher the revenues of the employer. It is true, and not false, therefore, that capital and labour are allies and not antagonistic forces, and that one cannot prosper when the other does not.

I feel as if I should apologise for taking so much space in stating truisms; but much of the prejudice and hostility which unnecessarily exist between capital and labour arise from such statements as those quoted.

To return to Mr. Gladstone. Would that his adhesion to "The Gospel of Wealth" in its entirety could be obtained! Deeply gratifying is the favour which he accords in general to its scope and aim; but the destructive character of his criticism upon one vital point is important. He is quite right in saying that, "though partial, it is a serious difference." It arises from his fond clinging affection for the principle of hereditary transmission of position and wealth, and of business, and for magnificence upon the part of those in station. We must meet this serious matter at the threshold.

The fundamental idea of "The Gospel of Wealth" is that surplus wealth should be considered as a sacred trust to be administered by those into whose hands it falls, during their lives, for the good of the community. It predicts that the day is at hand when he who dies possessed of enormous sums, which were his and free to administer during his life, will die disgraced, and holds that the aim of the millionaire should be to die poor. It likewise pleads for modesty of private expenditure.

The most serious obstacle to the spread of such a gospel is undoubtedly the prevailing desire of men to accumulate wealth for the express purpose of bequeathing it to their children, or to spend it in ostentatious living. I have therefore endeavoured to prove that, at the root of the desire to bequeath to children, there lay the vanity of the parents, rather than a wise regard for the good of the children. That the parent who leaves his son enormous wealth generally deadens the talents and energies of the son, and tempts him to lead a less useful and less worthy life than he otherwise would, seems to me capable of proof which cannot be gainsaid. It is many years since I wrote in a rich lady's album, "I should as soon leave to my son a curse as 'the Almighty Dollar.' " Exceptions abound to every general rule, but I think not more exceptions to this rule than to others, namely—that "wealth is a curse to young men, and poverty a blessing"; but if these terms seem rather strong, let us state the proposition thus: that wealth left to young men, as a rule, is disadvantageous; that lives of poverty and struggle are advantageous. Mr. Gladstone asks:—

Is it too much to affirm that the hereditary transmission of wealth and position, in conjunction with the calls of occupation and of responsibility, is a good and not an evil thing? I rejoice to see it among our merchants, bankers, publishers: I wish it were commoner among our great manufacturing capitalists.

He also says:—

Even greater is the subject of hereditary transmission of land: more important and more difficult.

Mr. Gladstone does not favour entails of money, but adds:—

But is it another matter when in commerce, or in manufacture, or in other forms of enterprise, such for example as the business of a great publishing house, the work of the father is propagated by his descendants?

These passages imply that the hereditary transmission of wealth and position and of business are not detrimental—as I think them—but desirable: a good and not an evil thing. Let us take the first form, that of sons following the occupations of their fathers. Little, I think, does one know, who is not in the whirl of business affairs, of the rarity of the combined qualities requisite for conducting the business enterprises of to-day. The time has passed when business once established can be considered almost permanently secure. Business methods have changed; goodwill counts for less and less. Success in business is held by the same tenure, nowadays, as the Premiership of Britain—at the cost of a perpetual challenge to all comers. The fond parent who invests his son with imaginary business qualifications, and places him in charge of affairs—upon the successful management of which the incomes of thousands depend—incurs a grave responsibility. Most of the disastrous failures of the day arise from this very cause. It is as unjust to the son as to the community. Out of seven serious failures during a panic in New York, five were traced to this root. One of these sons is in exile to escape punishment for breaking a law which he did not clearly understand. I have joined with others in asking the President to pardon him—a step I have never taken before on behalf of any law-breaker, but in this case I consider the father, not the son, the guilty party. The duty of the head of a great enterprise is to interest capable assistants who are without capital, but who have shown aptitude for affairs, and raise these to membership and management. The banker who hands over his business to sons, because they are sons, is guilty of a great offence. The transmission of wealth and rank, without regard to merit or qualifications, may pass from one peer to another not without much, but without serious injury, since the duties are a matter of routine and seldom involve the welfare or means of others, but the management of business, never.

But assuming that business enterprises can be handed over properly in deference to hereditary claims, is it wise or desirable that they should be? I think not. The millionaire business man rates his vocation higher than I, who sees in it the best or highest, or even a desirable career for his sons. The sons of the wealthy have a right instinct which tells them that to engage in work where the primary object is gain is unworthy of those who, relieved from the necessity of earning a livelihood, are in a position to devote themselves to any of the hundred pursuits in which their time and knowledge can be employed primarily for the good of the community. The sons of the millionaire are to be regarded with approval who cannot be induced to take the absorbing and incessant interest in their father's business which is necessary to save it from ruin. The day is over when even the richest can play at business, as rich men's sons must almost invariably do. There are exceptions where the son shows tastes and decided ability which render him the natural successor; but these are rare, far too rare to take into account in estimating the value of a custom. This ability, moreover, should be proved in some other establishment than that of the father.

When we come to the hereditary transmission of land, Mr. Gladstone's words are most touching. He paints a lovely picture of the

wonderful diversity and closeness of the ties by which, when rightly used, the office of the landed proprietor binds together the whole structure of rural society, . . . that cohesion, interdependence, and affection of the *gens*, which is in its turn a fast compacting bond of societies at large.

But is this a picture of to-day? Has not that day passed also, except in a few instances such as that furnished by the late lamented Lord Tollemache, and upon a smaller scale by Mr. Gladstone himself, in that earthly paradise, Hawarden?

The cultivation of land is now a business conducted upon a commercial basis by independent men, whom the landed proprietor no longer leads, and who most fortunately can lead themselves. The American citizen, who is himself landlord, factor, tenant, and labourer, requiring from the land he owns and tills only the support of himself and family, has rendered impossible the maintenance of more than one class from the product of agricultural land anywhere in the world. Knowing the kind of citizen which this condition creates, and knowing also the character of the Scotch farmer, as evolved through the operation of long leases which make him practically independent—although in his case the magic power of ownership, which counts for so much, is still lacking—and estimating these classes as men and as citizens, I have no doubt that the balance of advantage, both to the individual and to the State, is largely in favour of the change. Should the abolition of primogeniture and entail come with the changes democracy is expected to inaugurate, large estates in Britain would probably be divided into farms and owned by the people. The history of Denmark in this particular might then be that of Britain; and the temptation which now exists to leave territorial domains to eldest sons would thus be removed, and with it one great obstacle to the adoption of "The Gospel of Wealth"—the desire, futile as vain, to found or maintain hereditary families.

Mr. Gladstone instances the Marquis of Salisbury succeeding to the office of Prime Minister, which office ten generations ago was filled by one of his ancestors, and asks: "Is not this tie of lineage a link binding him to honour and to public virtue?" Is not Mr. Gladstone unfortunate in naming Lord Salisbury in support of his views? I have always regarded him as a striking instance of the advantage of not being born to hereditary wealth and position. Like the great founder of the Cecils, Lord Salisbury himself was born a commoner; a younger son with a younger son's portion; and with the promptings of decided ability within him, he did everything in his power to prevent being narrowed and restricted by the smothering robes of rank and wealth. The laws of his country forced him to sink his individuality in a peerage, but for which English history might have told of a first and a second Cecil, as it tells of a first and a second Pitt—men too great to be obliterated as men, by any title. It is a sad descent in historical rank from "Cecil" to the "Marquis" of anything. The highest title which a man can write upon the page of history is his own name. Mr. Gladstone's will be there; Gladstone he is, Gladstone he will remain, even if he tried to make future generations lose his commanding personality in "the Dukedom of Clydesdale," or any title whatever. But who among his contemporaries in public life is to stand this supreme test of masterdom? There is room for one only in each generation. It is safe to predict that, whoever he be, he will resemble "Gladstone" in one essential feature: he will be of the people, free from the disadvantage of hereditary wealth and position, and stamp his name and personality upon the glittering scroll. "Disraeli" promised well for a time, but he fades rapidly into Beaconsfield—a shadow of a name. The title proves greater than the man.

As a "Saturday Reviewer," Robert Talbot Cecil (what a glorious name to lose!) had proved himself a power: it is a hundred to one that, had he been born to the hereditary title, he would have remained an obscure commonplace Marquis, resembling in this respect the many generations of Marquises of Salisbury which had followed each other, and whose noble history is comprised—and fully comprised—in *Burke's Peerage* in the three letters, *b, m, d.* The only man of his family from whom he can derive inspiration "binding him to honour and to public virtue," is the great original Cecil, and the founder of his own branch of the house, who, like himself, was a younger son, and had neither wealth nor rank. He did not even reach knighthood till late in his career. The great Cecil sprang from the people, and had none of the advantages which Mr. Gladstone, as I think wrongly, attributes to hereditary wealth and position. Lineage is, indeed, most important, but only the lineage of the immediate parents; for in each generation one half of the strain is changed. Fortunately for the high-placed ones of the earth, it is unnecessary for them to scrutinise the characters of their ancestors beyond the preceding generation. Happy for the royal children of Britain that they can dwell upon the virtues of father and mother, and stop there. Lord Salisbury, like many able men, perhaps, owes his commanding qualities to his mother, who was the daughter of a country gentleman—a commoner, secure from the disadvantages of the hereditary transmission of wealth and rank. It is curious that the present ruler of the other branch of the English race, our President, has the same good fortune Mr. Gladstone claims for the Marquis of Salisbury, his grandfather having been President. But it is safe to say that the ruler upon this side would never have occupied that high office had he received fortune and position from his grandfather, or had he himself acquired riches. No party is so foolish as to nominate for the Presidency a rich man, much less a millionaire. Democracy elects poor men. The man must have worked for his bread to be an available candidate; and if, like Lincoln, he has been so fortunate as to be compelled to split rails, or, like Garfield, to drive mules upon a canal, and subsequently to clean the rooms and light the fires of the school in part payment for his tuition, or, like Blaine, to teach school, so much more successfully does he appeal to the people. This applies not only to the Presidency: one of the strongest aspirants for that office lost his renomination to the Senate, because a house that he erected in Washington was taken as an indication of tastes incompatible with republican simplicity of life. Nothing more fatal to the prospects of a public man in America than wealth, or the display of wealth. The dangers of a plutocracy that his Eminence Cardinal Manning fears are, I assure him, purely imaginary. There is no country in which wealth counts for so little as in the Republic. The current is all the other way. Is the influence of lineage less upon the Republican President in binding him to honour and public virtue, because neither hereditary rank nor wealth was transmitted? Because he is poor and a commoner, is he less sensitive to the promptings of honour and virtue? I think it will be found that the best and greatest of Britain do not differ from the greatest and best of other lands: these have had a lineage which linked them to honour and to public virtue, but almost without exception the lineage of honest poverty—of laborious wage-receiving parents, leading lives of virtuous privation, sacrificing comforts that their sons might be kept at school—lineage from the cottage of poverty, not the palace of hereditary rank and position. Mr. Gladstone himself has a lineage. Does it bind him less than Lord Salisbury is bound by his, to honour and public virtue? His ancestors were Scotch farmers without wealth or rank, yet I doubt not that Mr. Gladstone's career has been as strongly and as nobly influenced by his knowledge or recollections of the poor and virtuous lives lived by his forefathers, as that of any hereditary monarch or noble who ever lived could be by thoughts of his ancestors; and of one thing I am absolutely sure, he has reason to be much prouder of his lineage than nobles or monarchs in general can possibly be of theirs. Among many advantages arising, not from the transmission of hereditary wealth and position, but from the transmission of hereditary "poverty and health," there is one which, to my mind, overweighs all the others combined. It is not permitted the children of king, millionaire, or noble to have father and mother in the close and realising sense of these sacred terms. The name of father, and the holier name of mother, are but names to the child of the rich and the noble. To the poor boy these are the words he conjures with; his guides, the anchors of his soul, the objects of his adoration. Neither nurse, servant governess, nor tutor has come between him and his parents. In his father he has had tutor, companion, counsellor, and judge. It is not given to the born millionaire, noble, or prince to dwell upon such a heritage as is his who has had in his mother nurse, seamstress, teacher, inspirer, saint—his all in all.

Hereditary wealth and position tend to rob father and mother of their children, and the children of father and mother. It cannot be long ere their disadvantages are felt more and more, and the advantages of plain and simple living more clearly seen.

Poor boys reared thus directly by their parents possess such advantages over those watched and taught by hired strangers, and exposed to the temptations of wealth and position, that it is not surprising they become the leaders in every branch of human action. They appear upon the stage, athletes trained for the contest, with sinews braced, indomitable wills, resolved to do or die. Such boys always have marched, and always will march, straight to the front and lead the world; they are the epoch-makers. Let one select the three or four foremost names, the supremely great in every field of human triumph, and note how small is the contribution of hereditary rank and wealth to the short list of the immortals who have lifted and advanced the race. It will, I think, be seen that the possession of these is almost fatal to greatness and goodness, and that the greatest and the best of our race have necessarily been nurtured in the bracing school of poverty—the only school capable of producing the supremely great, the genius.

Upon the plea made by "The Gospel of Wealth" for modesty of private expenditure, Mr. Gladstone says:—

On which, however, it may be observed that among those whose station excuses or even requires magnificence, there are abundant opportunities, and there are also beautiful and graceful examples of personal simplicity and restraint.

This seems to me a branch from the Upas Tree of hereditary transmission of wealth and position. Is it true that station requires magnificence, or true that true dignity of station is enhanced by simplicity? Here are some words of President Cleveland in his message to Congress upon this point:—

We should never be ashamed of the simplicity and prudential economies which are best suited to the operation of a Republican form of government and most compatible with the mission of the American people. Those who are selected for a limited time to manage public affairs are still of the people, and may do much by their example to encourage, consistently with the dignity of their official functions, that plain way of life which among their fellow-citizens aids integrity and promotes thrift and prosperity.

President Cleveland only follows the teachings and examples of every American President, and of all others in official station. There are no pecuniary prizes in the Republic for judge, bishop, or president; neither any pensions except that judges are retired upon half-pay at seventy years of age. The very moderate salaries given to all officials enforce modest expenditure, and the influence of this upon the nation is as powerful as salutary. Were some future King of Britain to announce that the serious consideration of the subject of wealth and poverty had led him to resolve to live as the President of the United States and his family live, upon ten thousand pounds a year, and to return to the nation, or devote to public uses, the hundreds of thousands of pounds spent for magnificence, and were he to live in accordance with this resolve, would it lessen or enhance the true dignity of his life and station? Would it lessen or enhance his influence? Is it reasonable to estimate that all the good that monarch could possibly do in his restricted position would equal that which would flow from setting the example of living a quiet unostentatious modest life—administering his surplus not upon himself, but for others? The only objection that might be raised against such action is that it would render the king a personage far too powerful for the system of constitutional monarchy, which requires "king" to be but a word meaning the will of the Cabinet. The man capable of taking such action would not be only titular "king" but a power in the State. The Right Hon. John Morley, replying to a question asked by a constituent at a meeting in Newcastle, some time ago, bearing upon this very point of expenditure and magnificence in the State, gave expression to the hope that the highly placed might learn that the truest dignity consisted in quiet and simple living. I do not quote his words but the scope of his reply. Mr. Gladstone himself will leave behind him many titles to the affection, gratitude, and admiration of his countrymen; but when the future eulogist says of him—as he will truly be able to say—what is said of Pitt upon his monument in Guildhall, he will pay him the greatest of all tributes. These words are: "Dispensing for many years the favours of his sovereign, he lived without ostentation and died poor." If we cannot have Mr. Gladstone preaching in favour of modest living upon the part of those in station, we rejoice that none excels him in the practice of that virtue. It is seldom we are permitted to extol the example beyond the precept of the sage.

Upon this subject I thank Mr. Hughes for the words he has written. He says: "The real question is not how much we ought to give away, but how much we dare retain for our own gratification." These words strike home to every man of wealth and station: "How much *dare we retain* for our own gratification?" This is a troublesome question which will not "down." Giving the one-tenth—the tithe—is easy. The true disciple of "The Gospel of Wealth" has to pass far beyond that stage. His conscience may be quieted by arguing that he and his family are entitled to enjoy in moderation the best that the world affords. The earnest disciple can easily discover the efficacy of running in debt, as it were, by anticipating the expected surplus, and engaging in works for the general good before the cash is in hand, to an extent which really keeps him without available surplus, and even entails the necessity of figuring how to meet engagements. He can, when so situated, consider himself poor, and he will certainly feel himself so. The personal expenditure of the very rich forms so small a part of their income, provided the rule is obeyed which forbids such extravagance as would render them conspicuous, that they can, perhaps, also find refuge from self-questioning in the thought of the much greater portion of their means which is being spent upon others. But I do not profess that this is entirely satisfactory, and I am glad to agree with Mr. Hughes in the very low estimate he places upon this partial treatment of the serious question he has raised: "How much *dare we retain* for our own glorification?"

Upon the subject of giving, Mr. Gladstone thinks that I am severe in my judgment of private charity, when I estimate that of every thousand dollars spent in so-called charity, nine hundred and fifty of them had better be thrown into the sea. The history of the Charity Organisation of New York is here most instructive. Its confidential monthly bulletin recently gave the names of twenty-three bogus organisations which were soliciting contributions, many of them, unfortunately, with success. These have their printed annual reports, lists of distinguished contributors—in many cases, alas! these are genuine—their lady collectors, and all the other details. When the various charitable societies first combined and compared lists of those receiving aid, it was found that many names were upon seven or eight of the lists. Did my space permit, a story could be told that would impress upon every wealthy person that his duty is not to resolve to give, but to withhold until certain that his aid will not increase the area of what is called, in the stirring language of the day, "the hell of want and misery," which he longs to remove. The towns of Connecticut have recently been getting light upon almsgiving; a morning paper says:—

The experience of Hartford with well-to-do public beggars may be duplicated in almost every town in Connecticut. A year or two ago in Norwich, a town agent investigated the condition of the numerous persons who were receiving town aid. In forty instances he found that the applicants for charity had from $500 to $3,000 in the savings bank: in one case, that of a woman, who had been drawing "town money" for years, it was found she had nearly $20,000 in a local bank.

This is the least deplorable side of the matter, for the money given to prudent, saving people, even if they may not need it, cannot produce the serious consequences of that given to the much more numerous class who use it for the gratification of vice, and to enable them to live in idleness. Unless the individual giver knows the person or family in misfortune, their habits, conduct, and cause of distress, and knows that help given will help them to help themselves, he cannot act properly; and, if he does act to save his own feelings—which one is very apt to do—he will increase rather than diminish the distress which appeals to him. There is really no true charity except that which will help others to help themselves, and which does not place within the reach of the aspiring the means to climb. I notice a prevalent disposition to think only of the unfortunate wretches into whom the virtues necessary for improvement cannot be instilled. Common humanity impels us to provide for the actual wants of human beings to see through our poor laws, that none die of starvation, to provide comfortable shelter, clothing, and instruction which should, however, always be dependent upon work performed; but, in doing this, our thoughts should also turn to the benefits that are to accrue to those who are yet sound and industrious, and seeking through labour the means of betterment, by removing from their midst and placing under care of the State in workhouses the social lepers. Every drunken vagabond or lazy idler supported by alms bestowed by wealthy people is a source of moral infection to a neighbourhood. It will not do to teach the hardworking industrious man that there is an easier path by which his wants can be supplied. The earnest reformer will think as much, if not more, of the preservation of the sound and valuable members among the poor, as of any real change which can be effected in those who seem hopelessly lost to temperance, industry, and thrift. He will labour more to prevent than to cure, feeling that it is necessary to remove the spoiled grape from the bunch, the spoiled apple from the barrel, mainly for the sake of the sound fruit that remains. He who would plunge the knife into the social cancer, if any good is to be effected thereby, must needs be a skilled surgeon with steady hand and calm judgment, with the feelings as much under control as possible, the less emotion the better. One reads or hears everywhere of rash proposals, well-meaning no doubt, full of the innocence of the dove, but there is no task which more requires the wisdom of the serpent, which seems woefully lacking in these sensational schemes. The following from Rabbi Adler must be quoted; it is sound to the core (p. 889):—

Giving, however, is an easy matter; it needs neither special training nor sustained thought. But the purpose and methods of charitable relief cannot be learned without a long and diligent apprenticeship, for which discipline in the painful school of personal experience is alone of any avail.

Sorry as I am to say it, the more attention I give to this subject, the greater the genuine knowledge obtained, the higher I am disposed to raise my estimate of the evil produced by indiscriminate giving.

From the standpoint of "The Gospel of Wealth" Mr. Gladstone's criticisms are, indeed, serious—almost fatal—for it will be readily seen that if the hereditary transmission of wealth and position and of business concerns be not pernicious, as a rule, as I hold, but advantageous to the individuals receiving these bequests, and to the nation as well; and if station requires magnificence instead of simplicity, as I think, it will be hard indeed, if not impossible, to teach the wealthy that surplus wealth should be regarded as a sacred trust to be administered during their lives for the public good; they will continue to gather and leave fortunes to their families, or spend them for magnificence as hitherto. I turn, therefore, for support to the views of the other contributors; let us hear them.

His Eminence Cardinal Manning says:—

Mr. Carnegie tells us plainly, first, that the accumulation of stagnant wealth to be bequeathed to heirs is a vain-glory in the giver, and may be a ruin to the receiver; secondly, that the bequeathing of wealth for charities when the man is gone out of life is an empty way of making a name for generosity; thirdly, that to *distribute all, beyond the reasonable and temperate reserves due to kindred and their welfare, inter vivos, or now in life,* with his own will, judgment, and hand, to works of public and private beneficence and utility, is the highest and noblest use of wealth. This is a gospel, not according to capital, but according to the mind and life of the Founder of the Christian world. It is nothing new. It is no private opinion or exorbitant notion of a morbid prodigality, but the words of soberness and truth. If men so acted they would change the face of the world.

Mr. Hughes (p. 897):—

In the long and arduous task of reconstructing society on a Christian basis, with due and careful regard to all legitimate existing interests, it would be an inestimable public service if everyone whom Mr. Carnegie represents would follow the example of Mr. Carnegie in getting rid of his money as quickly as possible. Mr. Carnegie's "Gospel" is the very thing for the transition period from social heathenism to social Christianity. If a man is so unfortunate as to have enormous wealth, he cannot do better than act upon Mr. Carnegie's distributive principles.

I cannot but express the hope that further reflection upon the vital points may bring Mr. Gladstone into closer agreement with our colleagues in the discussion. In none of their articles is there a word in support of the advantages of the hereditary transmission of wealth and position, or of the necessity for magnificence upon the part of those in station. Their views seem to be in quite the other direction.

Fortunately, from this point forward, we have Mr. Gladstone's powerful and unreserved support. He says: "The accumulation of wealth has had adversaries, but it has been too strong for them all; it is the business of the world." "The Gospel of Wealth" advocates leaving free the operation of laws of accumulation. It accepts this condition as unassailable, and seeks to make the best of it by directing into new and better channels the streams of accumulated and accumulating wealth, which it is found impossible to prevent. But in this, while we have Mr. Gladstone with us, we have regretfully lost the Rev. Mr. Hughes, who rises in stern opposition and says:

"If 'Lay not up for yourselves treasures upon the earth' does not forbid the accumulation of wealth, the New Testament was written on Talleyrand's principle and was intended to 'conceal thoughts.' "

It is quite true, as Mr. Hughes says, "that expositors can prove anything, and that theologians can explain away anything." When applied to a rich man, his view of this very text—only part of which is quoted by Mr. Hughes—was that he strictly complied with the injunction, by always placing his treasures in the Safety Deposit Company, where he was quite sure "neither moth nor rust could corrupt, nor thieves break through and steal." Mr. Hughes quotes the parable of the "Master of the Vineyard" whose conduct is cited by Christ with approval. How came he master of a vineyard? Can he have sinned and "accumulated wealth" for the payment of labour? Mr. Hughes says: "Christ distinctly prohibited the accumulation of wealth." But when Christ spoke, the revenues of a leading minister, even if divided among the whole Twelve Apostles, would have been accounted "wealth." It seems to me we have only to interpret literally, in this manner, a few parts of isolated texts to find warrant for the destruction of civilisation. Five words spoken by Christ so interpreted, if strictly obeyed, would at one blow strike down all that distinguishes man from the beast: "Take no thought for tomorrow." There is reason to believe that the forces of Christianity are not thus to be successfully arrayed against the business of the world—the accumulation of wealth. The parable of the talents bears in the other direction. It was those who had accumulated, and even doubled their capital, to whom the Lord said: "Well done, thou good and faithful servant: thou hast been faithful over a few things, I will make thee ruler over many things: enter thou into the joy of thy Lord."

Those who had "laid up" their treasures and not increased them were reprimanded. Consider the millionaire who continues to use his capital actively in enterprises which give employment and develop the resources of the world. He who manages the ships, the mines, the factories, he cannot withdraw his capital, for this is the tool with which he works such beneficent wonders; nor can he restrict his operations, for the cessation of growth and improvement in any industrial undertaking marks the beginning of decay. The demands of the world for new and better things are continuous, and existing establishments must supply these, or lose even the trade they now have. I hope Mr. Hughes will find good ground for an interpretation which justifies the belief that the text has no bearing upon him, but is intended solely for those who hoard realised capital, adding the interest obtained for its use to the principal, and dying with their treasures "laid up," which should have been used as they accrued during the life of the individual for public ends, as "The Gospel of Wealth" requires. Acting in accordance with this advice it becomes the duty of the millionaire to increase his revenues. The struggle for more is completely changed from selfish or ambitious taint into a noble pursuit. Then he labours not for self, but for others; not to hoard, but to spend. The more he makes, the more the public gets. His whole life is changed from the moment that he resolves to become a disciple of "The Gospel of Wealth"; and henceforth he labours to acquire that he may wisely administer for others' good. His daily labour is a daily virtue. Instead of destroying, impairing, or disposing of the tree which yields such golden fruit, it does not degrade his life nor even his old age to continue guarding the capital from which alone he can obtain the means to do good. He may die leaving a sound business in which his capital remains; but beyond this, die poor, possessed of no fortune which was free for him to distribute, and therefore, I submit, not justly chargeable with belonging to the class which "lay up their treasures upon earth."

In this connection I commend to my reverend colleague the sermon of the founder of his Church (*The Use of Money*, vol. i, p. 44, Am. edition, sermon 50). He says:—

Gain all you can by honest industry. Use all possible diligence in your calling. Lose no time. Gain all you can, by common sense, by using in your business all the understanding which God has given you. It is amazing to observe how few do this; how men run on in the same dull track with their forefathers.

Having gained all you can by honest wisdom and unwearied diligence, the second rule of Christian prudence is, "Save all you can." Do not throw it away in idle expenses—to gratify pride, &c. If you desire to be a good and faithful steward, out of that portion of your Lord's goods which he has for the present lodged in your hands first provide things needful for yourself, food, raiment, &c. Second, provide these for your wife, your children, your servants, and others who pertain to your household. If then you have an overplus, do good to them that are of the household of faith. If there be still an overplus, do good to all men.

Upon this sermon "The Gospel of Wealth" seems founded. Indeed, had I known of its existence before writing upon the subject, I should certainly have quoted it. I shall, therefore, not be shaken, even if a leading disciple of Wesley informs us that Mr. Carnegie (as representing the millionaire class, of course) is an "anti-Christian phenomenon," a "social monstrosity," and a "grave political peril," and says, that "in a really Christian country—that is, in a country constructed upon a Christian basis—a millionaire would be an economic impossibility." The millionaire class needs no defence, although Mr. Hughes thinks it no longer of use since joint-stock companies provide the means for establishing industries upon the large scale now demanded. It is most significant that the business concerns which have given Britain supremacy are, with few or no exceptions, the creations of the individual millionaire: the Cunards, Ismays, Allens, Elders, Bessemers, Rothschilds, Barings, Clarks, Coates, Crossleys, the Browns, Siemens, Cammels, Gillotts, Whitworths, the Armstrongs, Listers, the Salts, Bairds, Samuelsons, Howards, Bells, and others. Joint-stock companies have not yet proven themselves equal to properly manage business after such men have created it. Where they have succeeded, it will be found that a very few individuals, and generally but one, have still control of affairs. Joint-stock companies cannot be credited with invention or enterprise. If it were not for the millionaire still in business leading the way, a serious check would fall upon future improvement, and I believe business men generally will concur in the opinion, which I very firmly hold, that partnership—a very few, not more than two or three men—in any line of business, will make full interest upon the capital invested; while a similar concern as a joint-stock company, owned by many in small amounts, will scarcely pay its way and is very likely to fail. Railroads may occur to some as examples of joint-stock management, but the same rule applies to these. America has most of the railroads of the world, and it is found whenever a few able men control a line, and make its management their personal affair, that dividends are earned, where before there were none. The railways of Britain being monopolies, and charging from two to three times higher rates for similar service than those of America, only manage to pay their shareholders a small return. It would be quite another story if these were the property of one or two able men and managed by them.

The "promotion" of an individual into a joint-stock concern is precisely what the "promotion" of the individual is from the House of Commons to the House of Lords. The push and masterdom, the initiative of the few owners, which have created the business, are replaced by the limited authority and regulation performance of routine duties by salaried officials, after "promotion," while the career of both concern and individual may continue respectable, it is necessarily dull. They are no longer in the race; the great work of both is over. It would not be well for Britain's future if her commercial and manufacturing supremacy depended upon joint-stock companies. It is her individual millionaires who have created this supremacy, and upon them its maintenance still depends. Those who insure steady employment to thousands at wages not lower than others pay, need not be ashamed of their record; for steady employment is, after all, the one indispensable requisite for the welfare and the progress of the people. Still I am neither concerned nor disposed to dispute Mr. Hughes's assertion that in a State under really Christian principles a millionaire would be an impossibility. He may be right; it is a far guess ahead. But the millionaire will not lack good company in making his exit; for surely nothing is clearer than that, in the ideal day, there can be no further use whatever for those of Mr. Hughes's profession. The millionaire and the preacher will alike have to find some other use for their talents; some other work to do that they may honourably earn and eat their daily bread. In this I doubt not both will continue to be eminently successful. The successors of the Rev. Mr. Hughes and myself, arm in arm, will make a pretty pair out in search of some light work with heavy pay.

Upon speculations as to the future of the race involving revolutionary change of existing conditions, it seems unwise to dwell. I think we have nothing whatever to do with what may come a thousand or a million years hence; and none of us can know what will come; our duties lie with the present—with our day and generation, and even these are hard enough to discern. The race toils slowly upward step by step; it has even to create each successive step before it can stand upon it, for

Nature is made better by no mean But nature makes that mean.

If it attempts to bound over intervening space to any ideal, it will not rise but fall to lower depths. I cannot therefore but regard such speculations a waste of time—of valuable time—which is imperatively required for dealing with the next step possible in the path upward. And it is in this light that Mr. Gladstone's suggestion is of the greatest value. It accepts and builds upon present conditions—accommodates itself to our present environments. Mr. Gladstone has been engaged during his long public career in focusing, as it were, the various wishes of others, and so grouping them for a common end that practical results might follow. It has been his mission to restrain extremes, and to unite in common action the advance, the centre, and the rear. He shows his rare constructive skill in suggesting that there should be formed a brotherhood of those who recognise their duties to their fellows less favoured with this world's goods. This society will, no doubt, be so wide as to admit all, no limit being put to the amount of percentage of his surplus which each can secretly resolve to devote to others, nor any interference attempted with the wide field of its application. We may expect kindred societies to be formed throughout the world, and, at intervals, delegates from these might meet together in one world-wide brotherhood, thereby strengthening each other in the desire and effort to do their best to improve the condition of the masses, and to bring rich and poor into closer union. Those who ask, "not how much we ought to give away, but how much we dare retain," would represent the advanced section. Passing from this through many gradations, those who still fondly plead for the continued hereditary transmission of wealth and position, and for magnificence in station, would constitute the other great wing of the army. All equally welcome, equally necessary—it being enough that members of the brotherhood feel the duty of the day is that, entrusted as they are with surplus wealth beyond their wants—as their conscience may determine these wants—they should regularly set apart and expend all, or a proportion greater or less of the remainder, for the good of their less fortunate fellows, in the manner which seems to each best calculated to promote their genuine improvement. Should Mr. Gladstone's suggestion find the response which it deserves, he will have added much to the usefulness of his life in a sphere happily far removed from and far above the political; a field in which there can be room neither for strife, jealousy, gain, nor personal ambition; a cause so high, so holy, that all its surroundings must breathe of peace, good-will, brotherhood!

Every earnest good man, anxious to leave the world a little better than he found it, will wish Mr. Gladstone God-speed in his new inspiring task—a task which is indeed "too great for haste, too high for rivalry."

THE GOSPEL OF WEALTH II

The problem of wealth will not down. It is obviously so unequally distributed that the attention of civilized man must be attracted to it from time to time. He will ultimately enact the laws needed to produce a more equal distribution. It is again foremost in the public mind to-day.

We have evidence of this in the President's recent speech (April 14th, 1906), in which he gives direct and forcible expression to public sentiment. We quote:

It is important to this people to grapple with the problems connected with the amassing of enormous fortunes, and the use of those fortunes, both corporate and individual, in business. We should discriminate in the sharpest way between fortunes well won and fortunes ill won; between those gained as an incident to performing great services to the community as a whole, and those gained in evil fashion by keeping just within the limits of mere law-honesty. Of course, no amount of charity in spending such fortunes in any way compensates for misconduct in making them. As a matter of personal conviction, and without pretending to discuss the details or formulate the system, I feel that we shall ultimately have to consider the adoption of some such scheme as that of a progressive tax on all fortunes beyond a certain amount, either given in life or devised or bequeathed upon death to any individual—a tax so framed as to put it out of the power of the owner of one of these enormous fortunes to hand on more than a certain amount to any one individual; the tax, of course, to be imposed by the national and not the State government. Such taxation should, of course, be aimed merely at the inheritance or transmission in their entirety of those fortunes swollen beyond all healthy limits.

It is seventeen years since the *North American Review* published "Wealth," written by the writer (republished September 21st, 1906), which strongly urged graduated taxation of estates at death of possessors as the easiest and best mode of insuring for the community a just share of great fortunes. He is in full accord with the President's views, as quoted, upon this vital question. Continued study has only confirmed him in his conviction of their justice, their beneficent effect upon society, and their necessity in the not-distant future. Much has been written of a contrary character. Graduated taxation has been denounced as unjust and Socialistic, fatal to Individualism and sure to sap the springs of enterprise. If the writer thought it favorable to Socialism or Communism, or in the least degree opposed to Individualism, he would be the last to favor it, for of nothing is he more fully convinced than that in Individualism lies the secret of the steady progress of civilization. Except we build upon the foundation of "As ye sow so shall ye reap," we labor in vain to establish a higher, or even to maintain the present, civilization. Virtue must bring reward, vice punishment, work wages, sloth misery. Energy and skill must win a prize denied to indolence and ignorance. He who sows the wind must reap the whirlwind.

The rights of private property emerged slowly from ages when property was held mostly in common; as civilization advanced men became less communistic and more individualistic. Public sentiment at last sustained private property because it was found favorable, and discarded Communism because it was found unfavorable, to progress; but there is nothing sacred about individual ownership except as man has established it as the system under which progress can be made. There is no cause to fear, therefore, that man is ever to turn round and creep backward toward the barbarism from which he has finally emerged. The law of evolution forbids, for his march is upward. Should he go too far in assessing wealth, he will inevitably reverse his action and adopt that policy which is best for the general good.

First, as to the justice of taxing large fortunes left at death upon a graduated scale for the benefit of the community. Graduated taxes are no new feature. Britain long since adopted them. They are advocated by no less an authority than Adam Smith, who says, "The subjects of every state ought to contribute to the support of government as nearly as possible in proportion to their respective abilities."

Let us go to the root of the matter and inquire how these fortunes are created, from whence and how they arise.

Imagine an honest hard-working farmer who finds himself able to give to each of his two sons a farm. They have married admirable young women of the neighborhood, of good kith and kin, friends from youth—no mistake about their virtues. The sons find farms, one in the centre of Manhattan Island, the other beyond the Harlem. They cast lots for the farms as the fairest method, thus letting the fates decide. Neither has a preference. The Harlem farm falls to the elder, the Manhattan to the younger. Mark now the problem of wealth, how it develops.

A few hundred dollars buy the farms, and the loving brothers set out for themselves. They are respected by all; loved by their intimates. To the extent of their means, they are liberal contributors to all good causes, and especially to the relief of neighbors who through exceptional troubles need friendly aid and counsel. They are equally industrious, cultivate their farms equally well and in every respect are equally good citizens of the state. Their children grow up and are educated together.

The growth of New York City northwards soon makes the children of the younger millionaires, while those of the elder remain simple farmers in comfortable circumstances, but still of the class who, fortunate in this beyond their cousins, have to perform some service to their fellows and thus earn a livelihood.

Now, who or what made this difference in wealth? Not labor, not skill. No, nor superior ability, sagacity, nor enterprise, nor greater public service. The community created the millionaire's wealth. While he slept, it grew as fast as when he was awake. It would have arisen exactly as it did had he been on the Harlem and his brother on the Manhattan farm.

The younger farmer, now a great property-holder, dies and his children in due time pass away, each leaving millions, since the farm has become part of a great city, and immense buildings upon it produce annual rents of hundreds of thousands of dollars.

When these children die, who have neither toiled nor spun, what canon of justice would be violated were the nation to step in and say that, since the aggregation of their fellow-men called "the community" created the decedent's wealth, it is entitled to a large portion of it as they pass away.

The community has refrained from exacting any part during their lives. The heirs have been allowed to enjoy it all, because although in their case the wealth was a purely communal growth, yet in other cases wealth often comes largely from individual effort and ability, and hence it is better for the community to allow such ability to remain in charge of fortune-making, because most likely to succeed, and in so doing develop our country's resources.

It would be unwise to interfere with the working bees; better allow them to continue gathering honey during their lives. When they die, the nation should have a large portion of the honey remaining in the hives; it is immaterial at what date collection is made, so that it comes to the National Treasury at last.

In a prosperous country, increasing rapidly in population, like our own, by far the greatest amount of wealth created in any department comes from enhanced values of real property.

The Census shows that from 1890 to 1900 the value of Real Estate increased from $39,544,544,333 to $52,537,628,164—an increase of $12,993,083,831.

The obvious creator of this wealth is not the individual but the community, as we see in the case of the two brother farmers. Property may pass through many proprietors, each paying more for it than his predecessor; but whether each succeeding owner sells to his successor at a profit depends almost solely upon whether the surrounding population increases. Let population remain stationary and so do values of property. Let it decline, and values fall even more rapidly. In other words, increased population—the community—creates the wealth in each successive generation. Decrease of population reduces it, and this law holds in the whole of that vast and greatest field of wealth, Real Estate. In no other field is the making of wealth so greatly dependent upon the community, so little upon the owner, who may wholly neglect it without injury. Therefore no other form of wealth should contribute to the nation so generously.

Let us now trace the acquisition of wealth by the active business man who has some personal part, and often not a small one, in creating it.

Imagine four brothers, sons of another hard-working farmer. The first settles in New York City, the second in Pittsburgh, the third in Chicago and the fourth in Montana. The first sees that railroads in every direction are essential to the coming Metropolis and devotes himself to this field, obtains large interests therein; and, as the population of the country increases and that of New York City bounds ahead into the millions, these lines of transport laden with traffic justify increasing bonded debt. Having the figures under his eye, he sees that the shares of these railways are sure to become dividend-paying, that even already there are surplus earnings beyond the bonded interest, which, if not needed for pressing extensions, could be paid in dividends and make the stock par. He strains his credit, borrows great sums, buys the shares when prices are low, and, floating upon a tidal wave of swelling prosperity, caused by the increased traffic of rapidly increasing communities, he soon becomes a multimillionaire and at his death his children are all left millionaires. In the consolidation of the various short lines into one great whole there was margin for a stupendous increase of capital; and in other collateral fields there lay numerous opportunities for profitable exploitation, all, however, dependent upon an expanding population for increased values. Now, while the founder of the family must be credited with remarkable ability and with having done the state some service in his day and generation, it cannot be denied that the chief creator of his wealth was the increasing communities along the railroads, which gave the traffic that lifted these lines into dividend-payers upon a capital far beyond the actual cost of the property.

In the work and its profits the Nation was an essential partner and equally entitled with the individual to share in the dividends.

The second son is so fortunate as to settle in Pittsburgh when it has just been discovered that some of the coal-fields of which it is the centre produced a coking-coal admirably adapted for iron-ore smelting. Another vein easily mined proved a splendid steam-coal. Small iron-mills soon sprang up. Everything indicated that here was indeed the future iron city, where steel could be produced more cheaply than in any other location in the world. Naturally, his attention was turned in this direction. He wooed the genius of the place. This was not anything extraordinarily clever. It was in the air. He is entitled to credit for having abiding faith in the future of his country and of steel, and for risking with his young companions not only all he had, which was little or nothing, but all they could induce timid bankers to lend from time to time. He and his partners built mills and furnaces, and finally owned a large concern making millions yearly. This son and his partners looked ahead. They visited other lands and noted conditions, and finally concluded that a large supply of raw materials was the key to permanent prosperity. Accordingly, they bought or leased many mines of iron ore, many thousands of acres of coal and of limestone and also of natural-gas territory, and at last had for many long years a full supply of all the minerals required to produce iron and steel. This was wise policy, but it did not require genius, only intelligent study and good judgment, to see that. They did not produce these minerals; they saw them lying around open for sale at prices that are now deemed only nominal. Much of the wealth of the concern came from these minerals which were once the public property of the community, and were easily secured by this fortunate son and his partners upon trifling royalties.

Their venture was made profitable by the demand for their products, iron and steel, from the expanding population engaged in settling a new continent. Without new populous communities far and near, no milliondom was possible for them. The increasing population was always the important factor in their success. Why should the Nation be denied participation in the results when the gatherers cease to gather and a division has to be made?

The third son was attracted to Chicago, and quite naturally became an employee in a meat-packing concern, in which he soon made himself indispensable. A small interest in the business was finally won by him, and he rose in due time to millionairedom, just as the population of the country swelled. If Chicago to-day, and our country generally, had only the population of early days, there could have been no great fortune for the third son. Here, as before, it was the magnitude of the business, based solely upon the wants of the population, that swelled the yearly profits and produced prodigious fortunes.

The fourth son, attracted by the stories of Hecla and Calumet, and other rich mines which "far surpass the wealth of Ormus or of Ind," settled in Montana and was lucky after some years of rude experience. His ventures gave him the coveted millionairedom. The amount of copper and silver required by the teeming population of the country and of other lands kept prices high, and hence his enormous profits mined from land for which only a trifle was paid to the General Government not so long ago. He did not create his wealth; he only dug it out of the mine as the demands of the people gave value to the previously worthless stones. Here especially we cannot but feel that the people who created the value should share the dividends when these must pass into other hands.

The fifth son had a melancholy career. He settled in New York City while young and unfortunately began his labors in a stock-broker's office, where he soon became absorbed in the fluctuations of the Exchange, while his fond mother proudly announced to all she met that he "was in business." From this the step was easy to taking chances with his small earnings. His gambling ventures proved successful. It was an era of rising values, and he soon acquired wealth without increasing values, for speculation is the parasite of business feeding upon values, creating none. A few years and the feverish life of the gamester told upon him. He was led into a scheme to corner a certain stock, and, as was to have been expected, he found that men who will conspire to entrap others will not hesitate to deceive their partners upon occasion if sure it will pay and be safe from exposure. He ended his life by his own hand. His end serves to keep his brothers resolute in the resolve never to gamble. The speculator seldom leaves a millionaire's fortune, unless he breaks down or passes away when his ventures are momentarily successful. In such a case, his ill-gotten gold should be levied upon by the state at the highest rate of all, even beyond that imposed upon Real Estate values. Wealth is often, we may say generally, accumulated in such manner as benefits the Nation in the process; here the means employed demoralizes the getter as well as the people, and lowers the standard of ethics. It is taken without returning any valid consideration.

There is one class of millionaires whose wealth in very much greater degree than others may be credited to themselves. Graham Bell of the telephone, Edison of numerous inventions, Westinghouse of the air-brake, and others, who originated or first applied processes hitherto unused, and were sufficiently alive to their pecuniary interests to hold large shares in the companies formed to develop and introduce them to the public. Their wealth had its origin in their own inventive brains. All honor to the inventor! He stands upon a higher platform than the others.

It may be said that in greater or less degree our leading manufacturers, railroad-builders, department-store projectors, meat-packers, and other specialists in one line or other had to adopt new methods; and, with few, if any, exceptions, there can be traced in their careers some special form of ability upon which their success depended, thus distinguishing them from the mass of competitors. No doubt this is correct, yet the inventions or processes used were the work of others, so that all they did was to introduce new methods of management or to recognize and utilize opportunities. This the inventor class have also done if they have become millionaires, but in addition they have invented the new processes. So that these deserve to reap beyond the other class, yet only in degree, because both classes alike depend upon increasing population—the masses, who require, or consume, the article produced, so that even the inventor's wealth is in great part dependent upon the community which uses his productions.

It is difficult to understand why, at the death of its possessor, great wealth, gathered or created in any of these or in other forms, should not be shared by the community which has been the most potent cause or partner of all in its creation. We have seen that enormous fortunes are dependent upon the community; without great and increasing population, there could be no great wealth. Where wealth accrues honorably, the people are always silent partners.

It is not denied that the great administrator, whether as railroad-builder, steamship-owner, manufacturer, merchant, banker, is an exceptional man, or that millions honestly made in any useful occupation give evidence of ability, foresight, and assiduity above the common and prove the man who has made them a valuable member of society. In no wise, therefore, should such men be unduly hampered or restricted as long as they are spared. After all, they can absorb comparatively little; and, generally speaking, the money-making man, in contrast to his heirs, who generally become members of the smart or fast set, is abstemious, retiring, and little of a spendthrift. The millionaire himself is probably the least expensive bee in the industrial hive, taking into account the amount of honey he gathers and what he consumes.

An Income Tax is sometimes proposed as one of the best possible modes of correcting the uneven distribution of wealth, but of all taxes this is the most pernicious. It demoralizes a Nation. Mr. Gladstone, one of the greatest financial ministers, advocated its abolition in Britain, alleging that it made a "Nation of Liars." During the Civil War, we had such a tax and paid it loyally, but public sentiment demanded its repeal and it was the first tax remitted when war ceased—justly so because it penalized the honest citizen. Its imposition would be strenuously opposed unless it were graduated and the exemption line placed high, so that the tax should be restricted to the few enormous fortunes. The Supreme Court has declared such a tax to be unconstitutional. No great gain would result to the state from it compared to what would accrue from the easier plan of exacting heavy taxes at death. The date of collection matters little, so that the payment is certain at last. Such proportions can be exacted as are deemed proper from time to time, unless it is generally agreed that great wealth at last pays its fair share to the people of the Nation, who were so highly instrumental in creating it or from whom it was gathered.

The collection of an Income Tax would require a large trained body of permanent officials to collect from indignant, discontented people, naturally resenting intrusive inquiries regarding their private affairs. The honest would always pay, the dishonest would usually escape. Much better that Corporations should be required to pay a dividend tax to the Nation which would be really a tax upon Incomes. It is by doing so that Britain realizes such enormous sums from its Income Tax. Were she to attempt to collect these direct from each individual, it would be found much less productive. So should we find if we made the attempt. There is no reason for so doing. Every dividend-paying Corporation can be made the rigid collector of Income Tax for the Government.

It is clearly at the rich man's death that the community should exact a large share of estate, a graduated share, increasing in proportion to its extent. It should be paid over to the Government and applied to the service of the people, the silent but contributive partner from whom it has been so largely derived. The graduated death duties exacted by Britain might guide us in the beginning. The maximum assessment upon estates to the lineal successors is eight percent upon the valuation, but to distant legatees it is very much higher. Smaller estates pay less in proportion.

Such contributions from the owners of enormous fortunes at death would do much to reconcile dissatisfied but fair-minded people to the alarmingly unequal distribution of wealth arising from the new industrial conditions of our day and the era of unprecedented prosperity our country has enjoyed for years.

The millionaire himself should rejoice at the thought of being a useful laborer in the national vineyard and in knowing that his contribution to the general fund at death will lessen the drain upon the scanty resources of his less successful fellows. Wealth left at death seldom does better service than this.

The people see how equivocally in many cases, how unfairly in others, fortunes have been made. Especially have the numerous failures of prominent men in official position to perform their duties properly deeply impressed them, and produced a strong feeling of antagonism to wealth and millionaires as a class. The appeal to them in the June number of this *Review* should not pass unheeded. As wealth comes mainly from the community, it should be administered as a sacred trust, by the temporary recipient, for the public good. Property in one sense is a mere creature of the law. Whether the holder be permitted to bequeath it to his successors and to what extent and how, are simply questions of policy for the people through the Government to determine. France has long restricted it. Our States generally designate the widow's share. There is here no question of right or wrong, but simply one of policy—what is best in all respects for the Nation.

Fortunes have recently been more easily made with us than ever, both in number and amount, with the inevitable result that sudden wealth is bound to produce in a new land, which, not so long ago, was much freer from immense fortunes than the older lands of Europe. Millionaires are a recent growth in the Republic. Multi-millionaires were unheard of before our day.

Some sixty-odd years ago, Britain, then in the beginning of the speculative period of railroad construction and manufacturing supremacy, had a somewhat similar experience. Greater fortunes were made than ever before; but the makers, imbued with the aristocratic ambition to become great landowners and county magnates, were soon absorbed into that class. They regarded wealth only as a means to an end—entrance to the aristocratic and fashionable circle. This refuge new millionaires lack under our democratic system, hence the vulgar, extravagant and offensive character of the follies to which they are driven, that evoke so much adverse criticism from people of education, good sense, and quiet respectable living, with whom mere dollars count for little. Funds collected by the Government from the estates of the millionaires at death would never be likely otherwise to be put to so good a use as the payment of Government expenditures, relieving the people in part from the burden of taxation.

We are yet as a nation in the heyday of youth. In time we shall tone down and live simpler lives and create different standards. Wealth will be dethroned as higher tastes prevail, its pursuit become less absorbing and less esteemed, and, above all, the mere man of wealth himself will come to realize that in the estimation of those of wisest judgment he has no place with the educated, professional man. He occupies a distinctly lower plane intellectually, and in the coming day Brain is to stand above Dollars, Conduct above both. The making of money as an aim will then be rated as an ignoble ambition. No man has ever secured recognition, much less fame, from mere wealth. It confers no distinction among the good or the great.

Meanwhile, as the masses become more intelligent, they may be expected to criticise and denounce the growth of fortunes which fail to contribute largely to the public good, and finally to insist that they shall be made to do so. The first step to this end should be heavy graduated death taxes upon wealth, in pursuance of Adam Smith's dictum already quoted.

Indications of alarm are sometimes seen regarding present conditions. Fears are expressed that a war of classes may arise. On the contrary, there are none but healthful signs in the awakening intelligence and deep interest of the masses in this problem. Its final solution upon right lines cannot but place the body politic in a much better position than before.

The American people can be trusted to deal with improper methods of business and excessive wealth accumulations wisely and well, to the advantage of the Nation, as they have met and solved other pressing problems, some of which for a time were thought by many likely to cause serious trouble, whereas the commotion only indicated that another step nearer the light was about to be taken. So will it be with this new problem of regulating, as needed, both corporations and individuals, that there may be fairer acquisition and fairer distribution of wealth.

WEALTH AND ITS USES

"Wealth," as Mr. Gladstone has recently said, "is the business of the world." That the acquisition of money is the business of the world arises from the fact that, with few unfortunate exceptions, young men are born to poverty, and therefore under the salutary operation of that remarkably wise law which makes for their good: "Thou shalt earn thy bread by the sweat of thy brow."

It is the fashion nowadays to bewail poverty as an evil, to pity the young man who is not born with a silver spoon in his mouth; but I heartily subscribe to President Garfield's doctrine, that "The richest heritage a young man can be born to is poverty." I make no idle prediction when I say that it is from that class from whom the good and the great will spring. It is not from the sons of the millionaire or the noble that the world receives its teachers, its martyrs, its inventors, its statesmen, its poets, or even its men of affairs. It is from the cottage of the poor that all these spring. We can scarcely read one among the few "immortal names that were not born to die," or who has rendered exceptional service to our race, who had not the advantage of being cradled, nursed, and reared in the stimulating school of poverty. There is nothing so enervating, nothing so deadly in its effects upon the qualities which lead to the highest achievement, moral or intellectual, as hereditary wealth. And if there be among you a young man who feels that he is not compelled to exert himself in order to earn and live from his own efforts, I tender him my profound sympathy. Should such a one prove an exception to his fellows, and become a citizen living a life creditable to himself and useful to the State, instead of my profound sympathy I bow before him with profound reverence; for one who overcomes the seductive temptations which surround hereditary wealth is of the "salt of the earth," and entitled to double honour.

One gets a great many good things from the New York *Sun*, the distinguished proprietor and editor of which you had recently the pleasure, benefit, and honour of hearing. I beg to read this to you as one of its numerous rays of light:

OUR BOYS

Every moralist hard up for a theme asks at intervals: What is the matter with the sons of our rich and great men? The question is followed by statistics on the wickedness and bad endings of such sons.

The trouble with the moralists is that they put the question wrong end first. There is nothing wrong with those foolish sons, except that they are unlucky; but there is something wrong with their fathers.

Suppose that a fine specimen of an old deerhound, very successful in his business, should collect untold deer in the park, fatten them up, and then say to his puppies: "Here boys, I've had a hard life catching these deer, and I mean to see you enjoy yourselves. I'm so used to racing through the woods and hunting that I can't get out of the habit, but you boys just pile into that park and help yourselves." Such a deerhound as that would be scorned by every human father. The human father would say to such a dog: "Mr. Hound, you're simply ruining those puppies. Too much meat and no exercise will give them the mange and seventeen other troubles; and if distemper doesn't kill them, they will be a knock-kneed, watery-eyed lot of disgraces to you. For heaven's sake keep them down to dog biscuit and work them hard."

That same human father does with great pride the very thing that he would condemn in a dog or a cat. He ruins his children, and then, when he gets old, profusely and sadly observes that he has done everything for them, and yet they have disappointed him. He who gives to his son an office which he has not deserved and enables him to disgrace his father and friends, deserves no more sympathy than any Mr. Fagin deliberately educating a boy to be dishonest.

The fat, useless pug-dogs which young women drag wheezing about at the end of strings are not to blame for their condition, and the same thing is true of rich men's sons. The young women who overfeed the dogs and the fathers who ruin their sons have themselves to thank.

No man would advocate the thing, perhaps; but who can doubt that if there could be a law making it impossible for a man to inherit anything but a good education and a good constitution, it would supply us in short order with a better lot of men?

This is sound. "If you see it in the *Sun* it is so." At least it is in this case.

It is not the poor young man who goes forth to his work in the morning and labours until evening that we should pity. It is the son of the rich man to whom Providence has not been so kind as to trust with this honourable task. It is not the busy man, but the man of idleness, who should arouse our sympathy and cause us sorrow. "Happy is the man who has found his work," says Carlyle. I say, "Happy is the man who has to work and to work hard, and work long." A great poet has said: "He prayeth best who loveth best." Some day this may be parodied into: "He prayeth best who worketh best." An honest day's work well performed is not a bad sort of prayer. The cry goes forth often nowadays, "Abolish poverty!" but fortunately this cannot be done; and the poor we are always to have with us. Abolish poverty, and what would become of the race? Progress, development would cease. Consider its future if dependent upon the rich. The supply of the good and the great would cease, and human society retrograde into barbarism. Abolish luxury, if you please, but leave us the soil, upon which alone the virtues and all that is precious in human character grow; poverty —honest poverty.

I will assume for the moment, gentlemen, that you were all fortunate enough to be born poor. Then the first question that presses upon you is this: What shall I learn to do for the community which will bring me in exchange enough wealth to feed, clothe, lodge, and keep me independent of charitable aid from others? What shall I do for a living? And the young man may like, or think that he would like, to do one thing rather than another; to pursue one branch or another; to be a business man or crafts-man of some kind, or minister, physician, electrician, architect, editor, or lawyer. I have no doubt some of you in your wildest flights aspire to be journalists. But it does not matter what the young man likes or dislikes, he always has to keep in view the main point: Can I attain such a measure of proficiency in the branch preferred as will certainly enable me to earn a livelihood by its practice?

The young man, therefore, who resolves to make himself useful to his kind, and therefore entitled to receive in return from a grateful community which he benefits the sum necessary for his support, sees clearly one of the highest duties of a young man. He meets the vital question immediately pressing upon him for decision, and decides it rightly.

So far, then, there is no difference about the acquisition of wealth. Every one is agreed that it is the first duty of a young man to so train himself as to be self-supporting. Nor is there difficulty about the next step, for the young man cannot be said to have performed the whole of his duty if he leaves out of account the contingencies of life, liability to accident, illness, and trade depressions like the present. Wisdom calls upon him to have regard for these things; and it is a part of his duty that he begin to save a portion of his earnings and invest them, not in speculation, but in securities or in property, or in a legitimate business in such form as will, perhaps, slowly but yet surely grow into the reserve upon which he can fall back in emergencies or in old age, and live upon his own savings. I think we are all agreed as to the advisability—nay, the duty—of laying up a competence, and hence to retain our self-respect.

Besides this, I take it that some of you have already decided, just as soon as possible to ask "a certain young lady" to share his lot, or perhaps his lots, and, of course, he should have a lot or two to share. Marriage is a very serious business indeed, and gives rise to many weighty considerations. "Be sure to marry a woman with good common sense," was the advice given me by my mentor, and I just hand it down to you. Common sense is the most uncommon and most valuable quality in man or woman. But before you have occasion to provide yourself with a helpmate, there comes the subject upon which I am to address you—"Wealth"—not wealth in millions, but simply revenue sufficient for modest, independent living. This opens up the entire subject of wealth in a greater or less degree.

Now, what is wealth? How is it created and distributed? There are not far from us immense beds of coal which have lain for millions of years useless, and therefore valueless. Through some experiment, or perhaps accident, it was discovered that black stone would burn and give forth heat. Men sank shafts, erected machinery, mined and brought forth coal, and sold it to the community. It displaced the use of wood as fuel, say at one-half the cost. Immediately every bed of coal became valuable because useful, or capable of being made so; and here a new article worth hundreds, yes, thousands of millions was added to the wealth of the community. A Scotch mechanic one day, as the story goes, gazing into the fire upon which water was boiling in a kettle, saw the steam raise the lid, as hundreds of thousands had seen before him; but none saw in that sight what he did—the steam engine, which does the work of the world at a cost so infinitely trifling compared with what the plans known before involved, that the wealth of the world has been increased one dares not estimate how much. The saving that the community makes is the root of wealth in any branch of material development. Now, a young man's labour or service to the community creates wealth just in proportion as his service is useful to the community, as it either saves or improves upon existing methods. Commodore Vanderbilt saw, I think, thirteen different short railway lines between New York and Buffalo, involving thirteen different managements, and a disjointed and tedious service. Albany, Schenectady, Utica, Syracuse, Auburn, Rochester, etc., were heads of some of these companies. He consolidated them all, making one direct line, over which your Empire State Express flies fifty-one miles an hour, the fastest time in the world; and a hundred passengers patronize the lines where one did in olden days. He rendered the community a special service, which, being followed by others, reduces the cost of bringing food from the prairies of the West to your doors to a trifling sum per ton. He produced, and is every day producing, untold wealth to the community by so doing, and the profit he reaped for himself was but a drop in the bucket compared with that which he showered upon the State and the nation.

Now, in the olden days, before steam, electricity, or any other of the modern inventions which unitedly have changed the whole aspect of the world, everything was done upon a small scale. There was no room for great ideas to operate upon a large scale, and thus to produce great wealth to the inventor, discoverer, originator, or executive. New inventions gave this opportunity, and many large fortunes were made by individuals. But in our day we are rapidly passing, if we have not already passed, this stage of development, and few large fortunes can now be made in any part of the world, except from one cause, the rise in the value of real estate. Manufacturing, transportation both upon the land and upon the sea, banking, insurance, have all passed into the hands of corporations composed of hundreds and in many cases thousands of shareholders. The New York Central Railroad is owned by more than ten thousand shareholders, the Pennsylvania Railroad is owned by more people than the vast army which it employs, and nearly one-fourth of the number are the estates of women and children. It is so with the great manufacturing companies; so with the great steamship lines; it is so, as you know, with banks, insurance companies, and indeed with all branches of business. It is a great mistake for young men to say to themselves: "Oh! we cannot enter into business." If any of you have saved as much as $50 or $100, I do not know any branch of business into which you cannot plunge at once. You can get your certificate of stock and attend the meeting of stockholders, make your speeches and suggestions, quarrel with the president and instruct the management of the affairs of the company, and have all the rights and influence of an owner. You can buy shares in anything, from newspapers to tenement-houses; but capital is so poorly paid in these days that I advise you to exercise much circumspection before you invest. As I have said to workingmen and to ministers, college professors, artists, musicians, and physicians, and all the professional classes: Do not invest in any business concerns whatever; the risks of business are not for such as you. Buy a home for yourself first; and if you have any surplus, buy another lot or another house, or take a mortgage upon one, or upon a railway, and let it be a first mortgage, and be satisfied with moderate interest. Do you know that out of every hundred that attempt business upon their own account statistics are said to show that ninety-five sooner or later fail. I know that from my own experience. I can quote the lines of Hudibras and tell you, as far as one manufacturing branch is concerned, that what he found to be true is still true to an eminent degree to-day:

Ay me! What perils do environ
The man that meddles with cold iron.

The shareholders of iron and steel concerns to-day can certify that this is so, whether the iron or steel be hot or cold; and such is also the case in other branches of business.

The principal complaint against our industrial conditions of to-day is that they cause great wealth to flow in to the hands of the few. Well, of the very few, indeed, is this true. It was formerly so as I have explained, immediately after the new inventions had changed the conditions of the world. To-day it is not true. Wealth is being more and more distributed among the many. The amount of the combined profits of labour and capital which goes to labour was never so great as to-day, the amount going to capital never so small. While the earnings of capital have fallen more than one-half, in many cases have been entirely obliterated, statistics prove that the earnings of labour were never so high as they were previous to the recent unprecedented depression in business, while the cost of living—the necessaries of life—have fallen in some cases nearly one-half. Great Britain has an income tax, and our country is to be subject to this imposition for a time. The British returns show that during the eleven years from 1876 to 1887 the number of men receiving from $750 to $2,500 per year increased more than 21 per cent., while the number receiving from $ 5 ,000 to $25,000 actually decreased 2- per cent.

You may be sure, gentlemen, that the question of the distribution of wealth is settling itself rapidly under present conditions, and settling itself in the right direction. The few rich are getting poorer, and the toiling masses are getting richer. Nevertheless, a few exceptional men may yet make fortunes, but these will be more moderate than in the past. This may not be quite as fortunate for the masses of the people as is now believed, because great accumulations of wealth in the hands of one enterprising man who still toils on are sometimes most productive of all the forms of wealth. Take the richest man the world ever saw, who died in New York some years ago. What was found in his case? That, with the exception of a small percentage used for daily expenses, his entire fortune and all its surplus earnings were invested in enterprises which developed the railway system of our country, which gives to the people the cheapest transportation known. Whether the millionaire wishes it or not, he cannot evade the law which, under present conditions, compels him to use his millions for the good of the people. All that he gets during the few years of his life is that he may live in a finer house, surround himself with finer furniture, and works of art which may be added; he could even have a grander library, more of the gods around him; but, as far as I have known millionaires the library is the least used part of what he would probably consider "furniture" in all his mansion. He can eat richer food and drink richer wines, which only hurt him. But truly the modern millionaire is generally a man of very simple tastes and even miserly habits. He spends little upon himself, and is the toiling bee laying up the honey in the industrial hive, which all the inmates of that hive, the community in general, will certainly enjoy. Here is the true description of the millionaire, as given by Mr. Carter in his remarkable speech before the Behring Sea tribunal at Paris:

Those who are most successful in the acquisition of property and who acquire it to such an enormous extent are the very men who are able to control it, to invest it, and to handle it in the way most useful to society. It is because they have those qualities that they are able to engross it to so large an extent. They really own, in any just sense of the word, only what they consume. The rest is all held for the benefit of the public. They are the custodians of it. They invest it; they see that it is put into this employment, that employment, another employment. All labour is employed by it and employed in the best manner, and it is thus made the most productive. These men who acquire these hundreds of millions are really groaning under a servitude to the rest of society, for that is practically their condition; and society really endures it because it is best for them that it should be so.

Here is another estimate by a no less remarkable man. Your friend, Mr. Dana, justly said at Cornell:

That is one class of men that I refer to, the thinkers, the men of science, the inventors; and the other class is that of those whom God has endowed with a genius for saving, for getting rich, for bringing wealth together, for accumulating and concentrating money, men against whom it is now fashionable to declaim, and against whom legislation is sometimes directed. And yet is there any benefactor of humanity who is to be envied in his achievements, and in the memory and the monuments he has left behind him, more than Ezra Cornell? Or, to take another example that is here before our eyes, more than Henry W. Sage? These are men who knew how to get rich, because they had been endowed with that faculty; and when they got rich, they knew how to give it for great public enterprises, for uses that will remain living, immortal as long as man remains upon the earth. The men of genius and the men of money, those who prepare new agencies of life, and those who accumulate and save the money for great enterprises and great public works, these are the leaders of the world, as the twentieth century is opening upon us.

The bees of a hive do not destroy the honeymaking bees, but the drones. It will be a great mistake for the community to shoot the millionaires, for they are the bees that make the most honey, and contribute most to the hive even after they have gorged themselves full. It is a remarkable fact that any country is prosperous and comfortable in proportion to the number of its millionaires. Take Russia, with its population little better than serfs, and living at the point of starvation upon the meanest fare—such fare as none of our people could or would eat—and you find comparatively few millionaires, excepting the Emperor and a few nobles who own the land. It is the same to a great extent in Germany, although in recent years industrial development has produced a few pound sterling millionaires. In Berlin in 1902 three had more than $6,000,000, and in Prussia six persons had an income of $1,000,000. In France, where the people are better off than in Germany, you can count but few millionaires. In the old home of our race, in Britain, which is the richest country in the world save one—our own— there are more millionaires in pounds sterling (which may be considered the European standard) than in the whole of the rest of Europe, and its people are better off than in any other. You come to our own land: we probably have more millionaires and multimillionaires, both in pounds and dollars, than all the rest of the world put together, although we have not one to every ten that is reputed so. I have seen a list of supposed millionaires, prepared by a well-known lawyer of Brooklyn, which made me laugh, as it did many others. I saw men rated there as millionaires who could not pay their debts. Some should have had a cipher cut from their reputed millions. Some time ago I sat next to Mr. Evarts at dinner, and the conversation touched upon the idea that men should distribute their wealth during their lives for the public good. One gentleman said that was correct, giving many reasons, one of which was that, of course, they could not take it with them at death.

"Well," said Mr. Evarts, "I do not know about that. My experience as a New York lawyer is that somehow or other they do succeed in taking at least four-fifths of it." Their reputed wealth was never found at death.

Whatever the ideal conditions may develop, it seems to me Mr. Carter and Mr. Dana are right. Under present conditions the millionaire who toils on is the cheapest article the community secures at the price it pays for him, namely, his shelter, clothing, and food.

The inventions of to-day lead to concentrating industrial and commercial affairs into huge concerns. You cannot work the Bessemer process successfully without employing thousands of men upon one spot. You could not make the armour for ships without first expending seven millions of dollars, as the Bethlehem Company has spent. You cannot make a yard of cotton goods in competition with the world without having an immense factory and thousands of men and women aiding in the process. The great electric establishment here in your town succeeds because it has spent millions and is prepared to do its work upon a great scale. Under such conditions it is impossible but that wealth will flow into the hands of a few men in prosperous times beyond their needs. But out of fifty great fortunes which Mr. Blaine had a list made of, he found only one man who was reputed to have made a large fortune in manufacturing. Fortunes are most often made from real estate; next follow transportation, banking. The whole manufacturing world furnished but one millionaire.

But assuming that surplus wealth flows into the hands of a few men, what is their duty? How is the struggle for dollars to be lifted from the sordid atmosphere surrounding business and made a noble career? Now, wealth has hitherto been distributed in three ways: The first and chief one is by willing it at death to the family. Now, beyond bequeathing to those dependent upon one the revenue needful for modest and independent living, is such a use of wealth either right or wise? I ask you to think over the result, as a rule, of millions given over to young men and women, and sons and daughters of the millionaire. You will find that, as a rule, it is not good for the daughters; and this is seen in the character and conduct of the men who marry them. As for the sons, you have their conditions as described in the extract which I read you from the *Sun*. Nothing is truer than this, that as a rule the "almighty dollar" bequeathed to sons or daughters by millions proved an almighty curse. It is not the good of the child which the millionaire parent considers when he makes these bequests, it is his own vanity; it is not affection for the child, it is self-glorification for the parent which is at the root of this injurious disposition of wealth. There is only one thing to be said for this mode: it furnishes one of the most efficacious means of rapid distribution of wealth ever known.

There is a second use of wealth, less common than the first, which is not so injurious to the community, but which should bring no credit to the testator. Money is left by millionaires to public institutions when they must relax their grasp upon it. There is no grace, and can be no blessing, in giving what cannot be withheld. It is no gift, because it is not cheerfully given, but only granted at the stern summons of death. The miscarriage of these bequests, the litigation connected with them, and the manner in which they are frittered away seem to prove that the Fates do not regard them with a kindly eye. We are never without a lesson that the only mode of producing lasting good by giving large sums of money is for the millionaire to give as close attention to its distribution during his life as he did to its acquisition. We have to-day the noted case of five or six millions of dollars left by a great lawyer to found a public library in New York, an institution needed so greatly that the failure of this bequest is a misfortune. It is years since he died; the will is pronounced invalid through a flaw, although there is no doubt of the intention of the donor. It is sad commentary upon the folly of men holding the millions which they cannot use until they are unable to put them to the end they desire. Peter Cooper, Pratt of Baltimore, and Pratt of Brooklyn, and others are the type of men who should be taken by you as your model; they distributed their surplus during life.

The third use, and the only noble use of surplus wealth, is this: That it be regarded as a sacred trust, to be administered by its possessor, into whose hands it flows, for the highest good of the people. Man does not live by bread alone, and five or ten cents a day more revenue scattered over thousands would produce little or no good. Accumulated into a great fund and expended as Mr. Cooper expended it for the Cooper Institute, it establishes something that will last for generations. It will educate the brain, the spiritual part of man. It furnishes a ladder upon which the aspiring poor may climb; and there is no use whatever, gentlemen, trying to help people who do not help themselves. You cannot push any one up a ladder unless he be willing to climb a little himself. When you stop boosting, he falls, to his injury. Therefore, I have often said, and I now repeat, that the day is coming, and already we see its dawn, in which the man who dies possessed of millions of available wealth which was free and in his hands ready to be distributed will die disgraced. Of course I do not mean that the man in business may not be stricken down with his capital in the business, which cannot be withdrawn, for capital is the tool with which he works his wonders and produces more wealth. I refer to the man who dies possessed of millions of securities which are held simply for the interest they produce, that he may add to his hoard of miserable dollars. By administering surplus wealth during life great wealth may become a blessing to the community, and the occupation of the business man accumulating wealth may be elevated so as to rank even with the physician, one of the highest of our professions, because he, too, in a sense, will be a physician, looking after and trying not to cure, but to prevent, the ills of humanity. To those of you who are compelled or who desire to follow a business life and to accumulate wealth, I commend this idea. The epitaph which every rich man should wish himself justly entitled to is that seen upon the monument to Pitt:

He lived without ostentation,
And he died poor.

Such is the man whom the future is to honour, while he who dies in old age retired from business, possessed of millions of available wealth, is to die unwept, unhonoured, and unsung.

I may justly divide young men into four classes:

First, those who must work for a living, and set before them as their aim the acquisition of a modest competence—of course, with a modest but picturesque cottage in the country and one as a companion "who maketh sunshine in a shady place" and is the good angel of his life. The motto of this class, No. 1, might be given as "Give me neither poverty nor riches."

"From the anxieties of poverty as from the responsibilities of wealth, good Lord, deliver us."

Class No. 2, comprising those among you are who determined to acquire wealth, whose aim in life is to belong to that much-talked-of and grandly abused class, the millionaires, those who start to labour for the greatest good of the greatest number, but the greatest number always number one, the motto of this class being short and to the point: "Put money in thy purse."

Now, the third class comes along. The god they worship is neither wealth nor happiness. They are inflamed with "noble ambition"; the desire of fame is the controlling element of their lives. Now, while this is not so ignoble as the desire for material wealth, it must be said that it betrays more vanity. The shrine of fame has many worshippers. The element of vanity is seen in its fiercest phase among those who come before the public. It is well known, for instance, that musicians, actors, and even painters—all the artistic class—are peculiarly prone to excessive personal vanity. This has often been wondered at; but the reason probably is that the musician and the actor, and even the painter, may be transcendent in his special line without being even highly educated, without having an all-around brain. Some peculiarities, some one element in his character, may give him prominence or fame, so that his love of art, or of use through art, is entirely drowned by a narrow, selfish, personal vanity. But we find this liability in a lesser degree all through the professions, the politician, the lawyer, and, with reverence be it spoken, sometimes the minister; less, I think, in the physician than in any of the professions, probably because he, more than in any other profession, is called to deal with the sad realities of life face to face. He of all men sees the vanity of vanities. An illustration of this class is well drawn in Hotspur's address:

By heavens, methinks it were an easy leap,
To pluck bright honour from the pale-faced moon;
Or dive into the bottom of the deep,
Where fathom-line could never touch the ground,
And pluck up drowned honour by the locks;

So he that doth redeem her thence might wear
Without corrival all her dignities.

Mark, young gentlemen, he cares not for use; he cares not for state; he cares only for himself, and, as a vain peacock, struts across the stage.

Now, gentlemen, it does not seem to me that the love of wealth is the controlling desire of so many as the love of fame; and this is a matter for sincere congratulations, and proves that under the irresistible laws of evolution the race is slowly moving onward and upward. Take the whole range of the artistic world, which gives sweetness and light to life, which refines and adorns, and surely the great composer, painter, pianist, lawyer, judge, statesman, all those in public life, care less for millions than for professional reputation in their respective fields of labour. What cared Washington, Franklin, Lincoln, or Grant and Sherman for wealth? Nothing! What cared Harrison or Cleveland, two poor men, not unworthy successors? What care the Judges of our Supreme Court, or even the leading counsel that plead before them? The great preachers, physicians, great teachers, are not concerned about the acquisition of wealth. The treasure they seek is in the reputation acquired through their service to others, and this is certainly a great step from the millionaire class, who struggle to old age, and through old age to the verge of the grave, with no ambition, apparently, except to add to their pile of miserable dollars.

But there is a fourth class, higher than all the preceding, who worship neither at the shrine of wealth nor fame, but at the noblest of all shrines, the shrine of service—service to the race. Self-abnegation is its watchword. Members of this inner and higher circle seek not popular applause, are concerned not with being popular, but with being right. They say with Confucius: "It concerneth me not that I have not high office; what concerns me is to make myself worthy of office." It is not cast down by poverty, neither unduly elated by prosperity. The man belonging to this class simply seeks to do his duty day by day in such manner as may enable him to honour himself, fearing nothing but his own self-reproach. I have known men and women not prominently before the public, for this class courts not prominence, but who in their lives proved themselves to have reached this ideal stage. Now, I will give you for this class the fitting illustration from the words of a Scotch poet who died altogether too young:

I will go forth 'mong men, not mailed in scorn,
But in the armour of a pure intent.
Great duties are before me, and great songs;
And whether crowned or crownless when I fall,
It matters not, so as God's work is done.
I've learned to prize the quiet lightning deed,
Not the applauding thunder at its heels,
Which men call fame.

Then, gentlemen, standing upon the threshold of life, you have the good, better, best presented to you—the three stages of development, the natural, spiritual, and celestial, they may fitly be called. One has success in material things of its aim—not without benefit this for the race as a whole, because it lifts the individual from the animal and demands the exercise of many valuable qualities: sobriety, industry and self-discipline. The second rises still higher: the reward sought for being things more of the spirit—not gross and material, but invisible; and not of the flesh, but of the brain, the spiritual part of man; and this brings into play innumerable virtues which make good and useful men.

The third or celestial class stands upon an entirely different footing from the others in this, that selfish considerations are subordinated in the select brotherhood of the best, the service to be done for others being the first consideration. The reward of either wealth or fame is unsought, for these have learned and know full well that virtue is its own and the only exceeding great reward; and this once enjoyed, all other rewards are not worth seeking. And so wealth and even fame are dethroned; and there stands enthroned the highest standard of all—your own approval flowing from a faithful discharge of duty as you see it, fearing no consequences, seeking no reward.

It does not matter much what branch of effort your tastes or judgment draw you to, the one great point is that you should be drawn to some one branch. Then perform your whole duty in it and a little more—the "little more" being vastly important. We have the words of a great poet for it, that the man who does the best he can, can whiles do more. Maintain your self-respect as the most precious jewel of all and the only true way to win the respect of others, and then remember what Emerson says, for what he says here is true: "No young man can be cheated out of an honourable career in life unless he cheat himself."

BUSINESS

Business is a large word, and in its primary meaning covers the whole range of man's efforts. It is the business of the preacher to preach, of the physician to practise, of the poet to write, the business of the university professor to teach, and the business of the college student, one might sometimes think, from the amount of attention bestowed upon it, to play football. I am not to speak of "business" in this wide sense, but specifically as defined in the *Century Dictionary*:

Mercantile and manufacturing pursuits collectively; employment requiring knowledge of accounts and financial methods; the occupation of conducting trade; or monetary transactions of any kind.

The illustration which follows is significant, and clearly defines this view of business. It reads:

It seldom happens that men of a *studious turn* acquire any degree of reputation for their knowledge of *business*.

But we must go one step further, more strictly to define business, as I am to consider it. Is a railway president receiving a salary, or the president of a bank, or a salaried officer of any kind, in business? Strictly speaking, he is not; for a man, to be in business, must be at least part owner of the enterprise which he manages and to which he gives his attention, and chiefly dependent for his revenues not upon salary but upon its profits. This view rules out the entire salaried class. None of these men is now a man in business, but many of them have been, and most successful therein. The business man pure and simple plunges into and tosses upon the waves of human affairs without a life-preserver in the shape of salary; he risks all.

CHOICE OF A CAREER

There is no great fortune to come from salary, however high, and the business man pursues fortune. If he be wise he puts all his eggs in one basket, and then watches that basket. If he is a merchant in coffee, he attends to coffee; if a merchant in sugar, he attends to sugar and lets coffee alone, and only mixes them when he drinks his coffee with sugar in it. If he mine coal and sell it he attends to the black diamonds; if he own and sail ships, he attends to shipping, and he ceases to insure his own ships just as soon as he has surplus capital and can stand the loss of one without imperilling solvency; if he manufacture steel, he sticks to steel, and severely lets copper alone; if he mine iron-stone, he sticks to that, and avoids every other kind of mining, silver and goldmining especially. This is because man can thoroughly master only one business, and only an able man can do this. I have never yet met the man who fully understood two different kinds of business; you cannot find him any sooner than you can find a man who thinks in two languages equally and does not invariably think only in one.

Subdivision, specialization, is the order of the day.

EVERY MAN TO HIS TRADE OR HIS SPECIALTY

I have before me many representatives of all classes of students. If I could look into your hearts, I should find many differing ambitions; some aiming at distinction in each of the professions; some would be lawyers, some ministers, some doctors, some architects, some electricians, some engineers, some teachers, and each sets before him, as models, honoured names that have reached the highest rank in these professions. The embryo lawyers before me would rival Marshall and Story of the past, or Carter and Choate of the present; the preacher would be a Brooks or a Van Dyke; the physician a Janeway or a Garmany; the editor would be a Dana; the architect a Richardson, and, having reached the top of his darling profession, his ambition then would be satisfied. At least, so he thinks at present. With these classes I have nothing whatever to do directly to-day, because all these are professional enthusiasts. Nevertheless, the qualities essential for success in the professions being in the main the same which insure success in business, much that I have to say applies equally to you all.

There remain among you those who would sail the uncertain sea of business, and devote themselves to making money, a great fortune, so that you shall be millionaires. I am sure that while this may be chiefly in your thoughts, it is not all you seek in a business career; you feel that in it there is scope for exercise of great abilities, of enterprise, energy, judgment, and all the best traits of human nature, and also that men in business perform useful service to society.

I am to try to shed a little light upon the path to success, to point out some of the rocks and shoals in that treacherous sea, and give a few hints as to the mode of sailing your ship, or rowing your shell, whether, for instance, the quick or the slow stroke is surer to win in the long race.

THE START IN LINE

Let us begin, then, at the beginning. Is any would-be business man before me content in forecasting his future, to figure himself as labouring all his life for a fixed salary? Not one, I am sure. In this you have the dividing line between business and non-business; the one is a master, and depends upon profits; the other a servant, and depends upon salary. Of course, you have all to begin as servants with salary, but you have not all to end there.

You have some difficulty in obtaining a start, great difficulty as a rule, but here comes in the exceptional student. There is not much difficulty for him; he has attracted the attention of his teachers, who know many men of affairs; has taken prizes, he is head of his class; has shown unusual ability, founded upon characteristics which are sure to tell in the race; he has proved himself self-respecting, has irreproachable habits, good sense, method, untiring industry, and his spare hours are spent in pursuing knowledge, that being the labour in which he most delights.

One vital point more: his finances are always sound, he rigorously lives within his means, and last, but not least, he has shown that his heart is in his work. Besides all this, he has usually one strong guarantee of future industry and ambitious usefulness, he is not burdened with wealth; it is necessary that he make his own way in the world. He is not yet a millionaire, but is only going to be one. He has no rich father, or, still more dangerous, rich mother, who can, and will, support him in idleness should he prove a failure; he has no life-preserver, and therefore must sink or swim. Before that young man leaves college he is a marked man. More than one avenue is open for him. The door opens before he is ready to knock; he is waited for by the sagacious employer. Not the written certificate of his professor—for certificates have generally to be read, and are read within the lines—but a word or two spoken to the business man who is always on the lookout for the exceptional young graduate has secured the young man all that a young man needs—a start. The most valuable acquisition to his business which an employer can obtain is an exceptional young man; there is no bargain so fruitful for him as this.

It is, of course, much more difficult for only the average student; he has generally to search for employment, but finally he also gets a start.

OPENINGS TO SUCCESS

It is the career of the exceptional student which illustrates the pathway to success. We need not render ourselves anxious about him; he is all right. He has been thrown into the sea, but he does not need any life-preserver; he does not need to be coddled; he will swim; he was not born to be drowned, and you see him breast the waves year after year until he is at the head of a great business. His start, of course, is not at the head, he is at the foot; fortunately so, for that is the reason his progress has always been upward. If he had started high he would not have had the chance to make a continual ascent. It does not matter much how he starts, for the qualities in him are such as to produce certain effects in any field he enters. He goes forward upon a very small salary performing certain small uses, indeed, much smaller than he thinks himself capable of performing, but these he performs thoroughly.

Some day in some way something happens that brings him to the notice of his immediate superior. He objects to some plan proposed, and thinks it can be bettered in some way, or he volunteers to assist in a department other than his own; or, he stays, one day, later at his work than usual, or goes some morning sooner, because there was some part of the business that had not been entirely settled the night before, or there was something to start the next morning that he was afraid might not be ready or just right, and he "just goes down early to be sure." His employer has been somewhat anxious upon the same point, and he, too, goes down early that morning and finds his salaried young man showing that he does not work for salary alone; it is not solely an affair of "hire and salary" with him; he is not that kind of a young man; he is working for the success of the business. Or it may be that some day his employer proposes a certain mode of action in regard to a customer's account; perhaps the young man has started in the office, and has been asked to look after the credits, a most important part. His employers wish to close this credit, which, perhaps, would embarrass the customer. This young man, known to the customer, has had to visit his place occasionally in the course of business, collecting his accounts or trying to collect them, and the young man modestly says he is a splendid fellow, bound to succeed, does his business upon fair and wise methods, and only needs a little temporary indulgence to come out all right.

The employer has faith in the young man's judgment and ability, thinks it a rather strong suggestion for a clerk to make, but says to him: "You look out for this matter, and see that we do not lose; but, of course, we do not wish to injure one of our customers; if we can help him without risk we wish to do it." The young man takes the matter in hand, and results prove he was quite right; the customer becomes one of the very best of all their customers, and one that it would require a great deal to take away from the firm.

Or, perhaps, the bright young man may have noted the insurance policies upon the works, and their dates of expiration; he finds the fact has been overlooked—that some of the insurances have lapsed and are invalid. It is none of his business; he is not paid to look after the insurance of the firm; in one sense—the narrow sense—that is the business of some other man, but he ventures to call attention to the fact, and suggests that the premiums should be paid. But now mark the advantage of general reading and education. This young man has read the newspapers and reviews, and learns of several "sharp business practices" by which the insurer is sometimes defrauded of his insurance, and especially has he read of new methods and cheap plans of insurance. He suggests that it would be well to change this and that policy to another and very solid old company. You see, gentlemen, the business man of this day has to read, yes, and study, and go to the roots of many things, that he may avoid the pitfalls that surround business upon every side. He would not be an employer worth having that did not note what kind of a young man that was, although now in the humble guise of a clerk.

THE SECOND STEP UPWARD

Suppose he is an electrician or engineer, and comes from Sibley, which is a good place to come from. In the great manufacturing concern so fortunate as to secure his services he has to do with some humble branch of the work, but he discovers that there are a few boilers which are not quite safe, and that the engines or motors are built upon false mechanical principles, and are very wasteful of fuel, and that one of the engines will soon give trouble; there is a foundation under it upon which he finds that the contractor has not done honest work; or dropping into the works one night just to see that all is going well, perhaps he discovers that a man trusted by the firm has fallen into bad habits, and is not fit for duty, or perhaps is not on duty, and that an accident might thus happen. He feels it to be his duty to take action here and safeguard the business from the danger of an accident. He draws the plans which show some defects in the machinery, lays them before his employers with suggestions how to cure these, made upon the latest scientific principles that he had been taught in Sibley. The employer, of course, is very averse to spend money, and angry to learn that his machinery is not what it should be. But although his anger explodes and envelops the young man for a moment, he is not shooting at him; when the *débris* clears off he sits down and learns from the young man what a few thousand dollars now might save, and the result is that he tells the Sibley boy he wishes him to take up this subject and attend to it, and be sure to make all right.

Already that young man's fortune is almost as good as made. He could not hide his light under a bushel if he tried, and the coming business man is not excessively liable to that sin, and does not want to; he is business all over. There is no affectation or false modesty about him. He knows his business, and he feels fully conscious and proud of the fact that he knows it, and that is one of the many advantages Sibley gives him, and he is determined that his employer should not, at least upon that point, know less than he does. You must never fail to enlighten your employer. You cannot keep such a young man as that back; and this let me tell you, no employer wishes to keep him back. There is only one person as happy at finding this young man as the young man is in finding himself, and that is his employer. He is worth a million more or less, but of course, it would not be good for him to get it, while so young.

He has now made two steps upward. First, he has got a start, and, secondly, he has satisfied his employer that he renders exceptional service, a decisive step; as the French say, "he has arrived," and he is there to stay. His foot is upon the ladder; how high he climbs is his own affair. He is among the few within the very threshold of the whole business.

There is a good deal to be done after this, however. This young man has zeal and ability, and he has shown that he has also that indispensable quality —judgment; and he has shown another indispensable quality—that his heart is in the business; that no other cause takes him from it; that he pushes aside the very seductive temptations which surround young men, and concentrates his attention, his time, his efforts, upon the performance of his duties to his employer. All other studies, occupations, and all amusements are subordinate to the business, which holds paramount sway. His salary, of course, increases. If he has happened to engage with an employer who does not fully appreciate such services as he has rendered, and is ready to render, other employers have not failed to note that here is that rare article, the exceptional young man, in the service of their rival, and it is possible that our young hero may have to change employers. It does not often happen, but it does sometimes, that a young man has to do so. As a rule, the employer is only too thankful that such a young man has come to him, and he makes it his interest to remain. Confidence is a matter of slow growth, however, and it is a far cry from a high salary as a hireling into equality as a partner.

THE CRUCIAL QUESTION

Let us trace him a little further. This young man's services to the firm have been such as to render it necessary some day that he should visit his employer at his house. It is not long before many occasions arise which call the young man to the house where he is now favoured upon his merits by the household, and to whom his nature soon becomes known, and the master soon begins to ask himself whether he might not some day make him a partner, and then comes the question of questions: *Is he honest and true?* Let me pause here one moment. Gentlemen, this is the crucial question, the keystone of the arch; for no amount of ability is of the slightest avail without honour. When Burns pictured the Genius of Scotland in "The Vision," these marvellous words came to him:

> Her eye, ev'n turn'd on empty space,
> Beam'd keen wi' honour.

No concealment, no prevarication, no speculation, trying to win something for which no service is given; nothing done which, if published, would involve your shame. The business man seeks first in his partner "the soul of honour," one who would swerve from the narrow path even to serve him would only forfeit his confidence. Is he intelligent? Is he capable of forming a correct judgment, based upon knowledge, upon distant and far-reaching issues? Young men, yes, and old men also, sometimes marry in haste, which is very foolish in both classes. But there is this to be said for the partnership—it is rarely entered upon in a hurry. It is not one or two qualities which insure it, but an all-round character, desirable in many respects, highly objectionable in none, and with special ability in one or two.

We often hear in our day that it is impossible for young men to become owners, because business is conducted upon so great a scale that the capital necessary reaches millions, and, therefore, the young man is doomed to a salaried life. Now there is something in that view only so far as the great corporations are concerned, because an interest in these is only attainable by capital; you can buy so many shares for so many dollars, and as the class of young men I address are not willing to remain forever salaried men, but are determined sooner or later to become business men upon their own account, as masters, I do not believe that employment in a great corporation is as favourable for them as with private owners, because, while a young man can look forward to a large salary in their service, that is all to which he can aspire. Even the presidents of these corporations, being only salaried men, are not to be classed as strictly business men at all. How, then, can a young man under them be anything but a salaried man his life long?

WHERE TO LOOK FOR OPPORTUNITIES

Many a business which has long been successful as a partnership is put into a joint stock concern, and the shares are offered in the market, and professional men, guilelessly innocent of business, and, sometimes, women of a speculative turn, and, I am sorry to say, many times clergymen, and artists, are deluded into purchasing. The public buys the business, but they should have bought the man or men who made the business.

You remember the Travers story? A friend called Travers in to see a dog that he wished to buy to clear his conservatory of rats, and when the dog-fancier undertook to show him how this dog demolished these pests, one great, big old rat chased the dog. Travers's friend said to him:

"What would you do?"

Travers replied: "B-b-b-buy the rat."

The public often buys the wrong thing.

It would be an excellent study for you to read frequently the stock-lists of miscellaneous companies. You will find some of the newspapers give the lists, then note the par value of the shares and the price at which you may purchase them. It may be said that this par value is upon fictitious capital. That is so only in some instances; in manufacturing companies especially I think the reverse is the rule. The capital does not fully represent the cost of the properties.

But there are many corporations which are not corporations, many instances of partnership in which the corporate form has been adopted, and yet the business continues substantially as a partnership, and comparing such institutions with the great corporations whose ownership is here, there, and everywhere, we find a most notable difference. Take, for instance, the great steamship lines of the world. Most of these, as those of you who read well know, fail to make returns to their shareholders. The shares of some of the greatest companies have been selling at one-half and sometimes one-third their cost. These are corporations, pure and simple, but if we look at other lines engaged upon the same oceans, which are managed by their owners and in which, generally, one great business man is deeply interested, and at the head, we find large dividends each year and amounts placed to the reserve fund. It is the difference between individualism and communism applied to business, between the owners managing their own business as partners and a joint stock concern of a thousand shifting owners ignorant of the business.

The same contrast can be drawn in every branch of business, in merchandising, in manufacturing, in finance, in transportation by land as well as by sea. It is so with banks. Many banks are really the property of a few business men. These soon become the leading banks, and their shares are invariably quoted at the highest premium, especially if the president of the bank be the largest owner, as he is in many of the most remarkable cases of success. In such partnership corporations there is every opportunity for the coming business man to obtain ownership which exists in pure partnerships, for the owners of both manage affairs and are on the constant watch for ability.

Do not be fastidious; take what the gods offer. Begin, if necessary, with a corporation, always keeping your eye open for a chance to become interested in a business of your own. Remember every business can be made successful, because it supplies some essential want of the community; it performs a needed office, whether it be in manufacturing which produces an article, or in gathering and distributing it by the merchant; or the banker, whose business is to take care of and invest capital.

There is no line of business in which success is not attainable.

A SECRET OF SUCCESS

It is a simple matter of honest work, ability, and concentration. There is no question about there being room at the top for exceptional men in any profession. These have not to seek patronage; the question is, rather, how can their services be secured? and, as with every profession so in every line of business, there is plenty of room at the top. Your problem is how to get there. The answer is simple: conduct your business with just a little more ability than the average man in your line. If you are only above the average your success is secured, and the degree of success is in ratio to the greater degree of ability and attention which you give above the average. There are always a few in business who stand near the top, but there are always an infinitely greater number at and near the bottom. And should you fail to ascend, the fault is not in your stars, but in yourselves.

Those who fail may say that this or that man had great advantages, the fates were propitious, the conditions favourable. Now, there is very little in this; one man lands in the middle of a stream which he tries to jump, and is swept away, and another tries the same feat, and lands upon the other side.

Examine these two men.

You will find that the one who failed lacked judgment; he had not calculated the means to the end; was a foolish fellow; had not trained himself; could not jump; he took the chances. He was like the young lady who was asked if she could play the violin; she said she "did not know, she had never tried." Now, the other man who jumped the stream had carefully trained himself; he knew about how far he could jump, and there was one thing "dead sure" with him: he knew he could, at any rate, jump far enough to land at a point from which he could wade ashore, and try again. He had shown judgment.

Prestige is a great matter, my friends. A young man who has the record of doing what he sets out to do will find year after year his field of operations extended, and the tasks committed to him greater and greater. On the other hand, the man who has to admit failure and comes to friends trying to get assistance in order to make a second start is in a very bad position, indeed.

COLLEGE GRADUATES IN BUSINESS

The graduates of our colleges and universities in former years graduated while yet in their teens. We have changed this, and graduates are older, as a rule, when they enter upon life's struggle, but they are taught much more. Unless the young university man employs his time to the very best advantage in acquiring knowledge upon the pursuit which he is to make the chief business of his life, he will enter business at a disadvantage with younger men who enter in their teens, although lacking in university education. This goes without saying. Now, the question is: Will the graduate who has dwelt in the region of theory overtake the man who has been for a year or two in advance of him, engaged in the hard and stern educative field of practice?

That it is possible for the graduate to do so also goes without saying, and that he should in after life possess views broader than the ordinary business man, deprived of university education, is also certain, and, of course, the race in life is to those whose record is best at the end; the beginning is forgotten and is of no moment. But if the graduate is ever to overtake the first starter in the race, it must be by possessing stronger staying-powers; his superior knowledge leading to sounder judgment must be depended upon to win the race at the finish. A few disadvantages he must strenuously guard against: the lack of severe self-discipline, of strenuous concentration, and intense ambition, which usually characterize the man who starts before the habits of manhood are formed. The habits of the young man at college, after he is a man, and the habits of the youngster in the business arena are likely to differ.

There is another great disadvantage which the older man has to overcome in most successful business establishments. There will be found in operation there a strict civil-service system and promotion without favour. It is, therefore, most difficult to find admission to the service in any but the lowest grades. One has to begin at the foot, and this is better for all parties concerned, especially the young graduate.

The exceptional graduate should excel the exceptional non-graduate. He has more education, and education will always tell, the other qualities being equal. Take two men of equal natural ability, energy, and the same ambition and characteristics, and the man who has received the best, widest, most suitable education has the advantage over the other undoubtedly.

BUSINESS MEN AND SPECULATORS

All pure coins have their counterfeits; the counterfeit of business is speculation. A man in business always gives value in return for his revenue, and thus performs a useful function. His services are necessary and benefit the community; besides, he labours steadily in developing the resources of the country, and thus contributes to the advancement of the race. This is genuine coin. Speculation, on the contrary, is a parasite fastened upon the labour of business men. It creates nothing and supplies no want. When the speculator wins he takes money without rendering service, or giving value therefore, and when he loses, his fellow-speculator takes the money from him. It is a pure gambling operation between them, degrading to both. You can never be an honest man of business and a speculator. The modes and aims of the one career are fatal to the other. No business man can honestly speculate, for those who trust him have a right to expect strict adherence to business methods. The creditor takes the usual risks of business, but not those of speculation. The genuine and the counterfeit have nothing in common.

That 95 percent fail of those who start in business upon their own account seems incredible, and yet such are said to be the statistics upon the subject. Although it is said that figures will say anything, still it is a fact that the proportion is very great. Do not think that I wish to discourage you against attempting to be your own masters and having a business of your own; very far from it. Besides, the coming business man is not to be discouraged by anything that anybody can say. He is a true knight who says with Fitzjames:

If the path be dangerous known,
The danger self is lure alone.

The young man who is determined to be a business man will not be thwarted, neither will he be diverted into any other channel, and he is going to start and have a trial; he will "make a spoon or spoil a horn" trying to make it. He must go ahead and find it out. Time enough to confine yourself to a life-long bondage as mere receivers of a salary after you have tried business, and really discovered whether or no you are one of the gifted who possess all the necessary qualities.

I have tried to sketch the path of the exceptional graduate from salary to partnership. It is no fancy sketch; there is not a day that passes without changes in many firms which raise young men to partnership, and in every single city no first of January passes without such promotions. Business requires fresh young blood for its existence. If any of you are discouraged upon this point, let me give you two stories within my own experience, which should certainly cheer you.

A SKETCH FROM LIFE

There is a large manufacturer, the largest in the world in his line. I know him well, a splendid man who illustrates the business career at its best. Now like all sensible business men, as he grew in years he realized that fresh blood must be introduced into his business; that while it was comparatively easy for him to manage the extensive business at present, it was wise to provide for its continuance in able hands after he had retired. Rich men seldom have sons who inherit a taste for business. I am not concerned to say whether this is well or otherwise. Looking at the human race as a whole, I believe it is for good.

If rich men's sons had poor men's necessities, and hence their ambitious abilities, there would be less chance for the students of colleges than there is. It was not to any member of his family that this man looked for the new young blood. A young man in the service of a corporation had attracted his attention in the management of certain business matters connected with the firm. The young man had to call upon this gentleman frequently. The wise man did not move hastily in the matter. About his ability he was soon satisfied, but that covered only one point of many. What were the young man's surroundings, habits, tastes, acquirements? Beyond his immediate business, what was his nature? He found everything in these matters just as he would have it. The young man was supporting a widowed mother and a sister; he had as friends some excellent young men, and some older than himself; he was a student; he was a reader; had high tastes, of course; I need hardly say that he was a young gentleman highly self-respecting, the soul of honour, incapable of anything low or vulgar; in short, a model young man, and of course, poor—that goes without saying.

The young man was sent for, and the millionaire told him that he should like very much to try him in his service, and asked the young man if he would make the trial. The millionaire stated frankly what he was looking for—a young business man who might develop, and finally relieve him of much care. The arrangement was that he should come for two years as a clerk, subject to clerks' rules, which in this case were very hard, because he had to be at the factory a few minutes before seven in the morning. He was to have a salary somewhat larger than he had received, and if at the end of two years nothing had been said on either side, no obligations were woven, each was free. He was simply on trial. The young man proudly said he would not have it otherwise.

The business went on. Before the two years expired the employer was satisfied that he had found that exceedingly rare thing, a young business man. What a number of qualities this embraces, including judgment, for without judgment a business man amounts to nothing. The employer stated to the young man that he was delighted with him, pleased with his services, and expressed his joy at having found him. He had now arranged to interest him in the firm. But to his amazement the young man replied:

"Thanks, thanks, but it is impossible for me to accept."

"What is the matter? You suit me; do I not suit you?"

"Excuse me, sir, but for reasons which I cannot explain, I am to leave your service in six months, when my two years are up, and I intended to give you notice of this, that you might fill my place."

"Where are you going?"

"I am going abroad."

"Have you made any engagement?"

"No, sir."

"Do you not know where you are going?"

"No, sir."

"Nor what you are to do?"

"No, sir."

"Sir, I have treated you well, and I do think I am entitled to know the real reason. I think it is your duty to tell me."

The reason was dragged out of the young man. "You have been too good to me. I would give anything to be able to remain with you. You even invited me to your house; you have been absent travelling; you asked me to call often to take your wife and daughter to such entertainments as they wished to attend, and I cannot stand it any longer."

Well, the millionaire, of course, discovered what all of you have suspected, just what you would have done under the circumstances; he had fallen in love with the daughter. Now in this country that would not have been considered much of an indiscretion, and I do not advise any of you to fight much against it. If you really love, you should overlook the objection that it is your employer's daughter who has conquered, and that you may have to bear the burden of riches; but in the land of which I speak it would have been considered dishonourable for a young clerk to make love to any young lady without the parents' permission.

"Have you spoken to my daughter?" was the question. The young man scarcely deigned to reply to that.

"Of course not."

"Never said a word, or led her to suspect in any way?"

"Of course not."

"Well," he said, "I do not see why you should not; you are the very kind of son-in-law I want if you can win my daughter."

Very strange, but somehow or other the young lady did not differ from papa; he was the kind of husband she wanted. Now that young man is a happy business man to-day.

ROMANCE IN BUSINESS

I have another story which happened in another country. Both the fathers-in-law told me these stories themselves, and proud men they are, and proud am I of their friendship. You see business is not all this hard prosaic life that it is pictured. It bears romance and sentiment in it, and the greater the business, the more successful, the more useful, in my experience, there is found more romance and imagination. The highest triumphs even in business flow from romance, sentiment, imagination, particularly in the business of a world-wide firm.

The other story is so similar to the first that successful telling is impossible. You will all jump to the conclusion, and the details in these cases are nothing. It is as when I began to tell my young nephews about the battle of Bannockburn; there were the English, and there stood the Scotch.

"Which whipped, uncle?" cried the three at once—details unnecessary. But there was no battle in this case. I infer it was all settled by amicable arbitration.

I shall not tell it at length, as I did the other, but it is precisely the same, except that the young man in this other case was not employed except in the ordinary manner. The young man's services were needed, and he was employed. He finally became private secretary to the millionaire, and with equally fatal results. In this case, however, the father asked this exemplary and able young man to look after his sons during his absence. This necessitated visits to the residence at the country house, and sports and games with his sons. My friend forgot he had a daughter, and he should not have done this. When you become not only heads of business but heads of families, you should make a note of this, and not think your sons everything. The private secretary, who was requested to attend to the sons, somehow or other, getting his instructions verbally, seems to have understood them as having a slightly wider range. The daughter apparently needed most of his attention. But note this: These two young men won the confidence and captured the judgment and admiration of their employers— business men—first, and then fell in love with the daughters. You will be perfectly safe if you take matters in the same order of precedence.

VALUE OF A BUSINESS CAREER

Perhaps, I may be permitted, without going too far beyond the scope of my text, to make a few remarks upon the influence of a business career upon men, as compared with other pursuits.

First, then, I have learned that the artistic career is most narrowing, and produces such petty jealousies, unbounded vanities, and spitefulness as to furnish me with a great contrast to that which I have found in men of affairs. Music, painting, sculpture, one would think, should prove most powerful in their beneficent effects upon those who labour with them as their daily vocation. Experience, however, is against this. Perhaps, because the work, or the performance, of artists is so highly personal, so clearly seen, being brought directly before the public, that petty passions are stimulated; however that may be, I believe it will not be controverted that the artistic mind becomes prejudiced and narrow. But, understand, I speak only of classes and of the general effect; everywhere we find exceptions which render the average still more unsatisfactory. In regard to what are called the learned professions, we notice the effect produced by specialization in a very marked degree.

In the ministerial class this is not so marked in our day, because leaders in that great function permit themselves a wider range of subjects than ever before, and are dealing less with creeds and formulas and more and more with the practical evils and shortcomings of human life in its various phases. This naturally broadens the mind. It has been held that the legal profession must tend to make clear, but narrow, intellects, and it is pointed out that great lawyers have seldom arisen to commanding position and power over their fellows. This does not mean that men who study law become unsatisfactory legislators or statesmen and rulers. If it did, our country, of all others, should be in a bad way, because we are governed by lawyers. But the most famous Americans who have been great men were not great lawyers; that is, they have seldom attained the foremost rank in the profession, but have availed themselves of the inestimable advantage which the study of law confers upon a statesman, and developed beyond the bounds of the profession. We are reminded that the great lawyer and the great judge must deal with rules and precedents already established; the lawyer follows precedents, but the ruler of men makes precedents.

MERCHANTS AND PROFESSIONAL MEN

The tendency of all professions, it would seem, must be to make what is known as the professional mind clear, but narrow. Now what may be claimed for business as a career is that the man in business is called upon to deal with an ever-changing variety of questions. He must have an all-round judgment based upon knowledge of many subjects. It is not sufficient for the great merchant and business man of our day that he know his country well, its physical conditions, its resources, statistics, crops, waterways, its finances, in short, all conditions which affect not only the present, but which give him data upon which he can predict, with some degree of certainty, the future.

The merchant whose operations extend to various countries must also know these countries, and also the chief things pertaining to them. His view must be world-wide; nothing can happen of moment which had not its bearing upon his action—political complications at Constantinople; the appearance of the cholera in the East; monsoon in India; the supply of gold at Cripple Creek; the appearance of the Colorado beetles, or the fall of a ministry; the danger of war; the likelihood of arbitration compelling settlement—nothing can happen in any part of the world which he has not to consider. He must possess one of the rarest qualities—be an excellent judge of men—he often employs thousands, and knows how to bring the best out of various characters; he must have the gift of organization—another rare gift—must have executive ability; must be able to decide promptly and wisely.

Now, none of these rare qualities is so absolutely essential to the specialist in any branch or profession. He follows a career, therefore, which tends not only to sharpen his wits, but to enlarge his powers; different, also, from any other careers, that it tends not to specialization and the working of the mind within narrow grooves, but tends to develop in a man capacity to judge upon wide data. No professional life embraces so many problems, none other requires so wide a view of affairs in general. I think, therefore, that it may justly be said for the business career that it must widen and develop the intellectual powers of its devotee.

On the other hand, the professional career is immeasurably nobler in this: that it has not for its chief end the ignoble aim of money-making and is free from the gravest danger which besets the career of business, which is in one sense the most sordid of all careers if entered upon in the wrong spirit. To make money is no doubt the primary consideration with most young men who enter it. I think if you will look into your hearts you will find this to be true. But while this may be the first, it should not be the last consideration.

There is the great use which a man can perform in developing the resources of his country; in furnishing employment to thousands; in developing inventions which prove of great benefit to the race, and help it forward. The sucessful man of affairs soon rises above the mere desire to make money as the chief end of his labours; that is superseded by thoughts of the uses he performs in the line which I have just mentioned. The merchant soon finds his strongest feeling to be that of pride in the extent of his international operations; in his ships sailing every sea. The manufacturer finds in his employees, and in his works, in machinery, in improvements, in the perfection of his factories and methods his chief interest and reward. The profitable return they make is chiefly acceptable not because this is mere money but because it denotes success.

There is a romantic as well as prosaic side to business. The young man who begins in a financial firm and deals with capital invested in a hundred different ways—in bonds upon our railway systems, in money lent to the merchant and to the manufacturer to enable them to work their wonders— soon finds romance in business and unlimited room for the imagination. He can furnish credit world-wide in its range. His simple letter will carry the traveller to the farthest part of the earth. He may even be of service to his country in a crisis, as Richard Morris, the great merchant in Philadelphia, was to General Washington in the Revolutionary cause, or, as in our own day, our great bankers have been in providing gold to our Government at several crises to avert calamity.

THE VANISHED PREJUDICE AGAINST TRADE

If the young man does not find romance in his business, it is not the fault of the business, but the fault of the young man. Consider the wonders, the mysteries connected with the recent developments in that most spiritual of all agents—electricity—with its unknown, and, perhaps, even unguessed of powers. He must be a dull and prosaic young man who, being connected with electricity in any of its forms, is not lifted from humdrum business to the region of the mysterious. Business is not all dollars; these are but the shell—the kernel lies within and is to be enjoyed later, as the higher faculties of the business man, so constantly called into play, develop and mature. There was in the reign of militarism and barbarous force much contempt for the man engaged in trade. How completely has all this changed! But, indeed, the feeling was of recent origin, for if we look further back we find the oldest families in the world proud of nothing but the part they played in business. The woolsack and the galley still flourish in their coat-of-arms. One of the most—perhaps the most—influential statesman in England to-day is the Duke of Devonshire, because he has the confidence of both parties. He is the president of the Barrow Steel Company. The members of the present Conservative cabinet were found to hold sixty-four directorships in various trading, manufacturing, and mining companies. In Britain to-day not how to keep out of trade, but how to get in it, is the question. The President of the French Republic, a man with a marvellous career, has been a business man all his days. The old feeling of aversion has entirely gone.

You remember that the late Emperor of Germany wished to make his friend, the steel manufacturer, Krupp, a Prince of the empire, but that business man was too proud of his works, and the son of his father, and begged the Emperor to excuse him from degrading the rank he at present held as King of Steel. Herr Krupp's son, who has now succeeded to his father's throne, I doubt not, would make the same reply to-day. At present he is a monarch equal to his Emperor, and from all I know of the young King Krupp, just as proud of his position.

The old prejudice against trade has gone even from the strong-holds in Europe. This change has come because trade itself has changed. In old days every branch of business was conducted upon the smallest retail scale, and small dealings in small affairs breed small men; besides, every man had to be occupied with the details, and, indeed, each man manufactured or traded for himself. The higher qualities of organization and of enterprise, of broad views and of executive ability, were not brought into play. In our day, business in all branches is conducted upon so gigantic a scale that partners of a huge concern are rulers over a domain. The large employer of labour sometimes has more men in his industrial army than the petty German kings had under their banners.

It was said of old that two of a trade never agree; to-day the warmest friendships are formed in every department of human effort among those in the same business; each visits the other's counting-house, factory, warehouse; and are shown the different methods, all the improvements, new inventions, and freely adapt them to their own business.

Affairs are now too great to breed petty jealousies and there is now allied with the desire for gain the desire for progress, invention, improved methods, scientific development, and pride of success in these important matters; so that the dividend which the business man seeks and receives to-day is not alone in dollars. He receives with the dollar something better, a dividend in the shape of satisfaction in being instrumental in carrying forward to higher stages of development the business which he makes his life-work.

REWARDS OF A BUSINESS CAREER

I can confidently recommend to you the business career as one in which there is abundant room for the exercise of man's highest power, and of every good quality in human nature. I believe the career of the great merchant, or banker, or captain of industry, to be favourable to the development of the powers of the mind, and to the ripening of the judgment upon a wide range of general subjects; to freedom from prejudice, and the keeping of an open mind. And I do know that permanent success is not obtainable except by fair and honourable dealing, by irreproachable habits and correct living, by the display of good sense and rare judgment in all the relations of human life, for credit and confidence fly from the business man foolish in word and deed, or irregular in habits, or even suspected of sharp practice. There may be room for a foolish man in every profession—foolish as a child beyond the range of his specialty, and yet successful in that—but no man ever saw a foolish business man successful. If without sound, all-round judgment, he must fail.

The business career is thus a stern school of all the virtues, and there is one supreme reward which it often yields which no other career can promise: I point to noble benefactions which it renders possible. It is to business men following business careers that we chiefly owe our universities, colleges, libraries, and educational institutions, as witness Girard, Lehigh, Chicago, Harvard, Yale, Cornell, and many others.

What monument can a man leave behind him productive of so much good, and so certain to hand his name down to succeeding generations, hallowed with the blessings of thousands in each decade who have within its walls received that most precious possession, a sound and liberal education? These are the works of men who recognized that surplus wealth was a sacred trust, to be administered during the life of its possessor for the highest good of his fellows.

If, then, some business men may fall subject to the reproach of grasping, we can justly claim for them as a class what honest Thomas Cromwell claimed for the great cardinal, and say: "If they have a greed of getting, yet in bestowing they are most princely, as witness these seats of learning."

Milton Keynes UK
Ingram Content Group UK Ltd.
UKHW051556260524
443099UK00012B/380